Bob Sinfield is an actor, broadcaster and freelance waster.

He is a frequent contributor to BBC Radio 3's *Jazz Line-Up* and has hosted his own show on Jazz FM.

His previous books include *The Gag Trade: Misadventures in TV and Radio Comedy* (snappy title) and he has written articles, reviews and obituaries (so far, not his own) for *The Independent*, *Folk Roots*, *Jazz Express* and *The Listener*.

Bob first saw George Chisholm in the flesh at the Regal Theatre, Redruth when he (Bob) was small and George was rather bigger. They first met in the early 1990s at a lunch which led to the book you're about to read.

GENTLEMAN OF JAZZ

The life of George Chisholm (1915-97)

BOB SINFIELD

DOCTOR SIN UK

&

Lulu.com

CONTENTS

When I first saw George Chisholm in 1963, he was in a striped jersey, tight trousers and a George Robey hat. His face was grey and grey - it was meant to be black and white but that's 405 lines for you. When I first met him in 1990, the jersey had gone but mercifully the trousers remained.

It was a BBC producer's idea (they do occasionally have them) for me to tell George's life story for posterity - or more to the point, for prosperity. The result, *Gentleman of Jazz* has finally made it into the bookshops in time for George's centenary, so you - yes YOU, dear reader! - are the first to set eyes on the finished work in print.

George died in 1997 at the age of 82, but the Gentlemen of Jazz continued to play his compositions and arrangements, under the direction of Don Morgan and featuring the vocal talents of George's daughter Carole. Their CD, *Tribute To A Jazz*

Legend was released on the Upbeat label and is available at www.upbeat.co.uk.

My thanks go to Carole for her help with the photographs; trumpeter and friend Digby Fairweather for his constant encouragement (and moustache); Jeff Walden at BBC Written Archives for his help with the research; oh, and Graham Pass (that BBC producer) for having the idea in the first place.

This book is dedicated to the memory of George Chisholm and his wife Etta.

BOB SINFIELD

Freelance Waster,

June 2014.

Chapter One

A BILLY OR A DAN OR AN OLD TIN CAN?

...in which young Chisholm is born, gets older and learns the finer points of sectarian diplomacy.

I was born on the 29th of March, 1915, at the age of nought. They said it couldn't last and sure enough, I soon found myself getting older, like a lot of people in Glasgow, specially around the high-rise tenement area in Bridgeton where I lived with two parents (one of each sex) and eventually two brothers, Bert and Ronnie.

The more mathematically-minded reader will deduce that I was only three when the war ended. If I'd been a bit more patriotic, perhaps I would have lied about my age and joined up, but instead my earliest memories were of playing among the Bridgeton slag-heaps, a less-than-exotic blend of coal and assorted debris, surrounded by hordes of other neighbourhood kids whom nobody seemed to look after. You were lucky if you could get your head above that. I could, but only because we lived three flights up.

It wasn't so bad that you needed special breathing equipment to cope with the altitude, but being at the top of so many stairs did tend to make us unpopular with the street traders. The local coalman used to come round with his horse and cart, and he would sing his wares. Instead of shouting,

"One and fourpence ha'penny coal", he'd set the phrase to music (sort of) with a little reprise of "Co-o-al" at the end. Very tasteful. So my mum or dad would shove their head through the window and call,

"Two bags, please" (for some reason, they never sang that bit), whereupon the coalman would smile at the thought of a sale. The smile soon faded when he saw how far up he'd have to lug a ten hundredweight bag. I'm amazed he didn't sing back,

"You must be jo-o-king!"

For most kids round our way, parents were a novelty. I was never particularly close to either of mine, mainly because I'd barely see them except on Sundays. The poor blighters were always working, Dad as a universal grinder (don't ask me), Mum mainly as a seamstress although for a time she did run a little dairy until the routine of rising at 5 a.m. to get the supplies became too much. Not that she had to do the milking herself, you understand. There weren't a lot of cows in Bridgeton.

Of the two, my mother was the disciplinarian. She had to be: Dad was amazingly placid. But they both cared about us and I've them to thank for getting me involved in music. Virtually every child in the district was given piano lessons as soon as they were old enough to tell the keys from the lid, but most parents would save themselves the expense of long-term tutorage if things weren't progressing. Fortunately, I took to it and was far happier at the keyboard than mucking about in the slag-heaps playing low-budget footie with a screwed-up lump of paper for the ball.

The older kids played even stranger games. They were less keen on soccer itself than the sort of behaviour you get from the fans. But they didn't use Celtic or Rangers as the pretext for a punch-up: in Bridgeton, sectarian hatred was based on religion. I may have missed the Great War but I saw plenty of small ones.

From the relative safety of the third floor, I was able to observe rival gangs taking part in theological debates in which the weaker side would lose face, often literally. Even at a distance, it was chilling stuff. The Protestant contingent were referred to as the Billy Boys, after William of Orange. They even had a song with such inspired lyrics as,

"Hallo, hallo, We are the Billy Boys..." (Ivor Novello award-winning potential, for sure). This they used as marching music, accompanying their journey from Monteith Street to the predominantly Catholic stronghold in Norman Street. With still greater imagination, the RCs had been dubbed 'the Norman Conkers'. Stop me if this imagery gets too sophisticated.

Also known as the Dans, they too would march and anyone with a brain would keep clear on a Friday night because that was when it always happened. I'd watch from the bedroom window, petrified at the sight of these bare-chested lunatics (even in the depths of winter) brandishing bayonets, hatchets and fists, beating each other senseless...not that they had much sense to start with.

As well as the Friday evening ritual, there were strategic ambushes on saints' days. Come March the 17th, the Billy Boys would hang round the Catholic school gates, ready to give the Dans a Patrick's Day trouncing. This bloodshed would be greeted by huge cheers as if something wonderful had happened! Similarly, the day commemorating William of Orange saw the Dans handing out festive punishment to the Billies.

And that was just Protestants v. Catholics. If you were Jewish, you got it from both sides. In fact, the only thing that united the two warring factions was a common bond of anti-semitism. In those parts, we didn't have born-again Christians: this mob were more intent on making you wish you'd never been born the first time! Lads showing no outward sign of belonging to either camp could expect to be stopped in the street with the words,

"A Billy or a Dan or an old tin can?"

and if you gave the right answer, you won a prize: you got to stay in one piece. Quite why Jewish people were referred to as 'old tin cans' never became apparent. Perhaps because they got kicked around a lot but more probably it was the only rhyme the morons could find for Dan. Cole Porter, eat your heart out!

Providing the wrong response to this cryptic question won you a consolation prize of two weeks in hospital, but there were ways round it. Happily, I wasn't stopped and challenged that often. My parents were Protestants but only in their spare time. I dare say they were vaguely proud of their faith, but we weren't church-goers so I wasn't immediately identifiable as a Billy. This made it easier to duck the issue when I did get interrogated. With a skill for evasiveness that would have been the envy of any politician, I'd reply by asking,

"Well, which are you? I only want to be seen with the best."

This display of transparent crawling seemed to confuse them and, more often than not, I'd wheedle a response out of them before committing myself, then simply declare the same allegiance. A child of five could have seen through me, but fortunately these children were older and couldn't. I hope none of them reads this. They're probably still thugs, even at the age of ninety.

The Chisholm brothers in action (Ronnie on piano). Courtesy: Derby Telegraph

Chapter Two

UNDERNEATH THE PIANO

...in which the Chisholms trade up to a more desirable area and young George finds piano-playing a pain in the neck.

After the inter-denominational rough-and-tumble of Bridgeton, we moved to a land of comparative peace: the Gorbals. Granted, it wasn't wise to go parading through the streets kilted in the Chisholm family tartan (or any other design for that matter), but at least life and limb no longer depended on belonging to the right church. Besides, even if I had nursed a smouldering urge to do some kilted parading, I would hardly have had the time.

On top of my schoolwork, I was having to do extra piano practice. Unlike many parents of young would-be musicians, my mother and father actively encouraged me to head off in the direction of an 'artistic' future. They even got me involved in a children's pierrot concert troupe, The Merry Magnets.

The manager of the local cinema manfully took on the task of instructing us kids in the finer points of stagecraft, no mean feat in a company ranging in age from 11 to 14. The range of talent on offer was pretty wide too: we had two comedians, several singers and dancers and, for the comic songs, one lone pianist. But in the event of flu or other distractions, the lone pianist would snap into action as Superdep. If a comic went missing, suddenly I was the comic. If a dancer broke a bone or a singer broke a voice, in a flash, I was the dancer...or singer...or both! Have you ever tried waltzing and playing chopsticks?

Still, it put me on my own resources, which was just as well since it was that same cinema manager who gave me my next job, playing music for silent films. There was no script so I just had to watch the action and adjust the music accordingly. As luck would fail to have it, the piano was right by the screen, so inevitably I developed a semi-permanent crick in the neck after two or three hours nightly of sitting with my head tilted at an angle of sixty degrees. Mind you, at the time of playing, I felt no pain. All my concentration went into following the plot of the picture or the newsreel item in front of me - well, above me. So when the hero came on, I'd burst into a quick chorus of *I'll See You Again*. When the villain arrived, I'd do a passable impression of *A Night On The Bare Mountain* at speed...but what do you play for 'Prince Of Wales Opens Gorbals Public Baths'? What did I play? Something jaunty and uptempo. He was a very fast mover, the Prince of Wales.

Stiff necks and fast-moving Princes aside, I was happy to be earning £4 10s. a week at the age of fourteen. I was still at school so I'd go straight from there to the picture house. Looking back, I was probably a bit of a novelty item, bearing in mind the cliché image of the cinema accompanist was very much the Margaret Rutherford type.

At the time, I looked nothing like her but even so I dare say my school chums regarded me as something of a jessie, especially as I'd be practising the piano while they were out playing football.

As I said, my parents were very supportive of my musical leanings. In fact, my father was a part-time musician himself. By day he was a universal grinder - by night he was The Singing Drummer! It was a curious combination of skills, made all the more so by the fact that he was a rotten singer. In those pre-microphone days, he made his voice heard over the drums by means of a giant megaphone erected on a stand beside the kit. Quite where this monstrosity came from, it's hard to say. I don't remember any megaphone shops in the Gorbals so he can't have just gone into one and bought it. Maybe it was something he knocked up while he was universally grinding. It was almost as big as the bass drum itself which was one of those great Salvation Army jobs with a hole in the top so you could lower in a 30-watt bulb to light up the name of the trio on the front skin. We were The Clifford Trio. Why I'll never know: my father wasn't called Clifford...and I don't think my mother was.

Transport arrangements for The

Clifford Trio were really very simple: there weren't any. We'd have to make our way to whichever venue by bus or tramcar and it was up to the conductor whether or not we worked that night. If he wouldn't let us on laden with banjo, drums and megaphone-with-stand (to say nothing of the 30-watt bulb), that was it. And sometimes, the thumbs-down from the tramcar conductor would save me from an evening of purgatory trying to pick tunes out of a chronically disabled piano. One of the greatest drawbacks of being a keyboard player was that, until the fairly recent innovation of light-weight portable electric models, you couldn't take it with you. So you'd just have to rely on the object provided by the management, often covered in cigarette burns and hideously unmusical (the piano, not the management…most of the time).

If a piano is seriously out of tune, it can drop dramatically in pitch. This would make it well nigh impossible for the banjo player to fit chords, so usually I would have to transpose the thing into another key and regard it as a tone away (sometimes it really would be a full tone out). Often this would land you in interesting key signatures like B and F sharp, but whatever musical atrocities this caused, it certainly was good practice for me. There'd be no point in rehearsing beforehand because if a piano's that badly out of tune to start with, it'll do something different every time you use it. Instead, we'd have our rehearsal and performance all at once!

For The Clifford Trio, gigs were by no means regular. We were lucky to get any, and they tended to average out at about one a month. It was the ballroom circuit, playing popular tunes of the day and catering for the variety of dance styles in vogue. Each venue boasted a wall-mounted contraption telling the punter the tempo of whichever dance was imminent. It would simply bear the legend 'Waltz' or 'Foxtrot' or 'Quickstep' and at the end of the number, one of the band (usually the drummer) had to suffer the indignity of standing on a chair and turning the handle on this thing until the name of the next dance appeared. Perhaps it was the ever-cautious management's way of ensuring that couples knew which steps to adopt, even if they couldn't pick up any clues from the band.

The clientele in these joints were more the middle-aged marrieds than the frantic youths you get thrashing about on dance floors today (Acid House had yet to reach the Gorbals), although there were those who came to meet and mate. From my vantage point at the piano, I was able to fill in one or two gaps in my somewhat undernourished sex education but by and large it was all pretty genteel, especially when compared with the two ballrooms I went on to work at after leaving school.

One was the Tower, an evil place! Every Friday night with sickening regularity, the lights would go out and all hell would be let loose. When the lights came on again, there'd be bodies lying everywhere. Including mine. Using my position at the piano as a lookout post, I was able to spot trouble when it was no more than a gleam in some villain's soon to be blackened eye. With a deftness that improved with practice (and I got plenty of it), I would immediately slide under my instrument and remain there until the danger passed. No one could accuse me of bravery. Once the hooligan element had exhausted themselves and each other, they'd be ejected down some stone steps and a little, self-appointed MC in a muffler and a cap would come on and say,

"Carry on dancing, please"

in a brisk, jovial way that almost had you believing you'd dreamt the carnage of a few seconds before.

At the piano (or under it) might have been the safest spot in the house but there were times when it didn't seem like it. Not everyone respected the sanctity of the bandstand. One notorious character who frequented the Tower always used to bring an iron hook with him. He had to, it was attached to his arm. He was called Wingy and he introduced himself to me by shambling onto the stage right in the middle of a number and joining me in a duet. Now, Wingy's concept of piano virtuosity was a touch primitive. It consisted of banging hell out of a few keys with his hook, then shooting me a belligerent, what-are-you-going-to-do-about-it look. With the same brand of courage that took me under the piano on other tense occasions, I said,

"That was very good. That was excellent!" and he seemed to think,

"Nobody's ever said that to me before."

And as he wandered away pondering on this, I'll swear I detected a tear in his eye! The ultimate hard man was weeping at what he thought was my unbounded generosity. Then back he came, the hard man again, and offered me the greatest means of repayment by saying,

"If you have any trouble here, call for Wingy. I'll fix it."

Thank God I never had to take him up on it.

* * * *

My other 'residency' was at the Playhouse. As a ballroom, it was a cut above the Tower and we used to play on a band-stand with an overhanging balcony all the way round, but even there bodies would be thrown from above, drop thirty feet and bounce onto the dance floor, giving off a cloud of resin particles. Then these guys would get up, not having hurt themselves thanks to that miracle-working anaesthetic called drink, and hurl threatening abuse at their enemies upstairs. Talk about not knowing when you're beaten!

Then as now, order would be kept by a squad of burlies in tuxedos. At a ball-room named Barrowland (so-called because it was in the midst of a street-market area), they had a ring of bouncers right across the front of the bandstand and I'll never forget the little man who came up and tapped the bandleader on the shoulder. That was the last thing he did from a vertical position.

In a flash, these neanderthals threw him down the stairs. Lying there in a state of severe bedragglement, he just about found just about enough strength to say,

"All…I wanted. . .was a request."

The young GC, trying not to look like quiz-master Michael Miles.

Chapter Three

SLEEPY TIME DOWN SOUTH

...in which an offer of work leads to full-time idleness in the Big Smoke.

Anyone leafing through what I've scribbled so far might somehow get the impression that certain parts of Glasgow were a little rough. Of course, that was all a long time ago. Since it became the European City of Culture in 1990, things have changed. Now they don't head-butt you with a naked brow: they put a nice designer-label scarf on first.

I wouldn't say violence was a way of life in the Glasgow of the 20s, but it was one way of making a living if you were good enough. If kids like Benny Lynch hadn't been given the chance of a career in boxing, they might easily have ended up dying of drink on the slag-heaps. As it turned out, Benny had a formidable career in boxing and <u>still</u> ended up dying of drink on the slag-heaps. But for a time, he was real heroic material. I remember the great homecoming when he brought the World Flyweight Championship title to Glasgow. The entire city was ecstatic and Benny was feted all over the place.

I was particularly aware of this event because we were living just over the road from the Gorbals Jewish Institute, 122 South Portland Street (one of my favourite numbers). It was decided that they'd throw a celebration lunch for Benny there. There was just one problem: after all the plaudits that were lavished upon him, etiquette demanded that Benny should reply. A great pugilist he undoubtedly was, but coherent speech was not his forte. So some bright spark came up with the idea of letting Benny's manager speak on his behalf.

Accordingly, the manager staggered to his feet and with the best intentions in the world, said (this next bit to be read in broad Scottish),

"Well, we're delighted to bring this title back, so on behalf of Benny and myself, we must thank all youse Jews for this party!"

You can imagine the scene. It was almost as punch-packed as the title fight itself. Maybe Benny should have spoken after all.

$$* * * *$$

Gradually, I was learning about life. I'd left school at fourteen to become a professional musician (in the sense that I was getting paid for it) and the incidents so far related gave me a pretty thorough grounding in the ways of violence. And then there was sex. From the bandstand, I didn't miss many of the 'goings-on' and usually it was pretty easy to tell when two separate bodies were planning a merger. I'd watch in amazement as a fellow musician showed signs of taking a fancy to one of the dancers. Nothing was ever said. All that would pass between them, resulting eventually in 'intimacy', I suppose, would be a nod. The muso would incline his head in an interrogative sort of way and get an affirmative response from the lady. And that was it. Not even a hint of 'What was your name was again?'

I never got over my astonishment that something so intimate could occur just from a nod. Terrible. Dreadful. I'll be glad when I've had enough!

My own courting days had begun after meeting a local girl called Ella Tierney. A keen dancer, she used to enter competitions at the Playhouse ballroom, the ones where people wore numbers on their backs and you kept expecting to hear cries of 'Come in, number seven. Your time's up!'

Before long, I was a regular visitor to (and diner in) the Tierney household, just round the corner from us, where she lived with several sisters. I can't have been much more than twenty when Ella and I decided to get married. I was earning enough for us to afford a place of our own but we'd barely had time to get settled there before I was on the move.

By this time, I was playing trombone as well as piano...and as well as could be expected. It was fairly usual for musicians to tackle more than one instrument, though not at the same time (the likes of Roland

Kirk were still a thing of the future). For reasons best known to themselves, saxophonists would often double on fiddle of all things (can't be because the embouchure was the same) and conversely, any number of rhythm players took great pleasure in picking up front-line instruments. It was said to be every backing musician's dream to be out front. Pianists tended to be overshadowed and drowned out by the brass boys so who could blame us for wanting a bit more coverage?

My first choice of portable instrument was a trifle unorthodox: the accordion. Why I'll never know. I hadn't even heard Jack Emblow at the time. But my parents soon found themselves paying out for young George's accordion on the hire purchase. They might have guessed it was a fool's errand: within what seemed like seconds, young George got fed up with it. Apart from anything else, I was getting corns on my stomach! So it was back to the shop with it and pay off the odds. Never let it be said that I didn't know how to make myself popular at home.

After this somewhat extravagant but thoroughly false start, I opted for the trombone and had the sense to stick with it. I'd heard records by Jack Teagarden, a wonderful American player whom everyone I knew either slavishly copied or were heavily influenced by and I thought, 'That's for me!' - so the long-suffering parents helped me buy my first trombone. I got it in Edinburgh (a little place just outside Glasgow) where I'd been playing second piano at the West End Cafe in Princes Street. All I had to do then was learn how to play it.

I was given a course of twelve lessons by a man called Jimmy Chalmers. Jimmy was with the SCWS (Scottish Co-Operative) Brass Band, a very good player who always won the solo trombone prize and still found time to coach pupils every Sunday. I'd take the tram up to his house to be greeted with a cheery cry of

"Come in, son. Let's see what you can do."

and while I played through a few scales, he would reach into a drawer and pull out the most evil set of false teeth, slightly brown in character, followed by a tin of off-white powder which he'd proceed to sprinkle over the teeth before going through the nauseating motions of inserting both plates in his gob to the accompaniment of an ob-scene sucking sound. I was just praying he wouldn't ask me for a French kiss!

* * * *

One of the advantages of working at the Playhouse was that visiting bandleaders would look in for a bit of talent-spotting. Some of them were pretty big fish and the word quickly got round as to who was 'in' tonight. If the whisper had it that someone like Lew Stone was in the auditorium, you'd find all of us dusting off our best audition pieces and snatching furtive upward glances at the celebrity corner in the balcony, hoping to see some kind of positive re-action. I don't know what we were ex-pecting exactly. Maybe we thought Lew

34

was going to stand on a chair and hold up a card with marks out of ten on it.

Mind you, our dreams of being 'snapped up' weren't without foundation. Quite a lot of musicians did go on to bigger and better bands as a result of being seen there: trombonist Donald McAffer caught Lew Stone's ear to good effect while his trumpeting brother Jimmy was invited to join a band led by Teddy Joyce and, merciful heaven, so was I.

Teddy Joyce isn't a name that's as well remembered today as the likes of Lew Stone, Ambrose and Roy Fox, but he was a prominent and popular figure in the dance band era and going with him was definitely an upward move for me, even though it meant a lot of domestic disruption and a trip to that mythical place called London where I didn't know a soul. I felt sure it would be worth all the hassle, but sadly my predominant memory of that era is one of unemployment.

Having gone through the euphoria

of being spotted and signed by a major bandleader, I made the long train journey south only to discover that the orchestra was 'resting', a state of affairs which lasted some time. So there I was with a wife and home to support back in Glasgow, rent to pay for lodgings in London and little or no income. Once more, my valiant parents helped me through, supplementing my post office savings, but times were lean and so was I. It was a case of having to work out how many (or how few) meals you could manage on in a day. At that time, Lyons Corner House in Coventry Street was open all night. My first digs were in Brixton but there was a decent tram service up to the West End so, late mornings, I'd generally be found in Lyons, making the brunch last as long as possible, then going into pubs and eating all the freebies in bowls on the counter. My 'usual' would be a half of beer and six tons of almonds. Evenings would often be spent 'sitting in' at various clubs. I was happy about that because it gave me the chance to play, and the club owners were happy because it cost them nothing.

London was a shock to my system. I couldn't get over the amount of space there. From then on, whenever I went back to Glasgow, the old home city seemed so pokey in comparison. Also, the Scottish speech idioms became quite hard to follow through lack of practice. I was told quite bluntly that my voice had gone all posh and when asked why I'd changed the way I spoke, I usually replied that it was cheaper than travelling an interpreter. Really, I wasn't that bothered because it couldn't affect my playing: you don't hear many trombones with upper-class accents.

After staying in Brixton for a time, I transferred to the West End and moved into a large and antiquated boarding house very near the Cambridge Theatre in Covent Garden. The woman in charge was a cross between the archetypal theatrical landlady and the madam of a bordello. As far as I know, it wasn't what was then quaintly and coyly referred to as 'a house of ill repute' but a number of prostitutes did live there, along with members of what were known as 'race gangs' (people who worked at race-courses) and a kind of unholy bond existed among our three groups. If a muso or a hooker or someone from a race gang was in trouble, the others would rally to support them. It was a sort of low-life version of the Masons, although we were spared the indignity of rolling up our trousers.

You'll have gathered that work was a long time in coming for the Teddy Joyce band. Even when it did start to trickle through, financial corners were often cut. We'd be paid on turning up of a Saturday night and the usual question was 'How much can you do without?' I'd come into the band with a promise of five pounds and ten shillings a week, ten bob more than I was making at the Glasgow Playhouse, and eventually I worked my way up to a weekly tenner...in theory. The full whack was rarely forthcoming, though, and I tended to be fobbed off with seven quid and the promise of three more to come (I'm still waiting). Teddy's father didn't help matters much either. Don't ask me what his function was in the set-up. Perhaps he had a monetary interest because he spent all his time trying to beat us down to lower wages, coming out with arch expressions like 'Hitch your wagon to a star'. The essential requirements for dealing with Joyce senior were a lot of patience and a phrase-book.

Eric Whitley was our vocalist, but Teddy decided he didn't like that name so he saddled poor Eric with the toe-curling moniker of Tony Lombardo. This struck our leader as having a suitably romantic, open-necked shirt kind of ring to it. Tony (sorry, Eric) owned a motorbike which he used to travel between gigs and, on one occasion, he offered me a lift to a far-flung corner of Cleveland. Foolishly, I accepted. So there I was on the pillion for several hundred miles, wondering if I'd ever again get any feeling in my lower limbs. Eventually I pleaded with Eric to change places and, after much persuasion and overacting, he charily agreed. Just one problem: I'd never ridden a motorbike before. Still, I couldn't be doing with such trifling considerations. I quickly got the hang of small technical points like where to find the clutch and the accelerator, then off we roared.

Now, Eric was a tenor and I was treated to a private display of the top of his range as he spent much of the remaining journey screaming his head off. Good lyrics too: they seemed to consist largely of 'Stop! Stop! Stop!', a tad repetitive but catchy nonetheless. I suppose he had a point because one time when I looked round, we'd jack-knifed so badly that there he was, right beside me! I don't remember being offered a lift again.

Despite all the economic wrangles, Teddy's was a good band to be in. He had that quality of showmanship which a lot of the other leaders lacked. While Jack Hylton or Jack Payne would come across as very austere on the podium, Teddy would tear about the stage, a tall and imposing figure in a monkey suit, full of bright ideas about how to make the show more eye-catching for the punters. One of his most inspired tableaux, which looked very impressive out front, involved dividing the band into three rows with one lot kneeling, the second row crouching behind them and the others standing at the back, all bedecked in white gloves, some with black strips sewn in, and holding out their hands to resemble the three-layered keyboard of a giant organ. Teddy would stand in front and give the impression of playing the thing, all the appropriate noises being made in the right places. Well, mostly.

Visually, it was a great success but, musicians being what they are, the sound effects were sometimes augmented by outbreaks of flatulence from the back row. Few things can be worse than trying to hum accompaniment to a girl singer's gen-teel rendering of *The Bells of St. Clements* while some drunk's gaffing away in the middle distance. The sound alone was enough to produce such side-effects of suppressed laughter as trembling voices and heaving shoulders, but add to that the pungent atmosphere and you've got a bunch of grown men on the verge of collapse through hysteria. And the more Teddy spat 'How dare you! Don't do that!' at us, the worse we got. Still, having heard some of the sounds an organ's capable of making, maybe our sozzled chum wasn't so far off the mark.

A smoke-filled jam session with Keith Christie (trombone), Art Ellison (tenor sax) and Alan Clare at the piano.

Chapter Four

WALLERING IN NOSTALGIA

...in which the name of Chisholm is immortalised on wax by the Cheerful Little Earful.

Mention Thomas 'Fats' Waller and the phrase that leaps to mind is 'fast liver'. Sadly at the end, it was more a case of collapsed liver: Fats liked his juice to be on the strong side of lemonade.

He visited London in 1938 and a recording session organised by the jazz entrepreneur Leonard Feather brought together in EMI's Abbey Road studios seven backing musicians, colourfully dubbed the Continental Rhythm (yes, I know it sounds like an exotic contraceptive but people were a lot more innocent then). Among their number was a trombonist called Chisholm and for part of the day, a drummer called Edmundo Ros. I wonder whatever happened to him?

Although studio dates are never quite as sparky as live gigs, we couldn't help but have a wild time that day, thanks to Fats' personality which was almost as huge as his frame. Rather than be shy about his vastness, he was happy to joke about it, seating himself at the stool and asking,

"Is you all on, Fats?"

On top of the piano, almost as essential as the instrument itself, was his fuel. Fats' taste in whisky favoured a brand which managed to get itself a free plug on one of the takes. He had a little man with him whose job it was to look after his every want, mostly to see that the glass was replenished every so often. At one point, he must have been slacking because Fats called out,

"Hey man, gimme some more John Haig".

It's clearly audible on the disc, as is a reference to 'Brother Chisholm' - nice to know I ranked alongside Haig in importance.

The size of the man governed the way he played. He had huge hands: if you can imagine two ordinary-sized hands stuck together, that would be one of Fats Waller's. That weight throwing itself at the keyboard had the equivalent impact of about five pounds of meat and he was capable of producing such a hefty sound that he didn't really need a bass player. But there was far more to his performing skill than mere volume. He had the ability to take pretty much any popular song and give it new life just when you thought you'd never want to hear it again. Not for nothing was he known as 'the Cheerful Little Earful'.

He was a marvellous composer too, penning some memorable tunes like *Ain't Misbehavin'* (which we recorded that day), *Honeysuckle Rose* and *Blue Turning Grey Over You*, but he sold them all for a pittance in order to buy more bottles of the stuff he advertised on that session. Come to think, I've just advertised it too! And not a penny changed hands - so much for musicians' business sense.

After we left the studio, the music wasn't over as far as Fats was concerned and we ended up jamming in several clubs around London. He 'sat in' some of the time and drank almost all of the time. Of course, I did my fair share too but eventually the sauce got the better of Fats. In 1943, he was found dead in the compartment of a train as it pulled into New York City. I imagine his autopsy produced the same degree of surprise as did Charlie Parker's when the age of the deceased was revealed. Fats could have passed for 50, but he died at 39.

Still, there was no denying the youthful energy and sense of mischievous fun he injected into his work, and I was lucky enough to see first-hand that it was genuinely a part of him, not something he just switched on for the punters.

In fact, my luck had taken a general turn for the better after the ups, downs and sideways (but not in that order) of life in the Teddy Joyce ensemble. The late 30s proved to be a busy time in the studios (well, busier than the mid-30s), including a session with Benny Carter and Coleman Hawkins recorded in The Hague (as opposed to the Waller session which was recorded in the Haig).

Benny has often been referred to as 'King Carter' and there can be few better candidates for musical royalty. An arranger, composer and multi-instrumentalist (mainly alto saxophone and trumpet but he's also been heard on tenor sax, clarinet, trombone and piano!), his working life began in the 20s, the original Jazz Age, and continued through the many twists and turns of the music over subsequent decades, not just keeping pace but often being at the fore-front of the innovations; a complete musician capable of being both faultless and exciting, two factors that don't always go hand in hand.

The pre-war era found him in London, working with Henry Hall from the *Guest Night* of the same name (a popular weekly radio show). There seemed to be an unwritten clause in the contracts of visiting American musicians at the time that, come the end of the day job, they had to go down to the Nest Club in Kingly Street. Having made a habit of sitting in free of charge at various other jam joints of the day such as the exotically titled Palm Beach, the even more exotic Nuthouse and a place called Mother Hubbard's (these days it would probably be Freddie Hubbard's), I eventually got signed up at the Nest as part of the resident band, along with musos like the alto saxophonist Jock Myddleton, a huge baritone sax player named Derek Neville who eventually went off to be a taxi driver in Australia (he probably did well, it's a big place) and Duncan Whyte, the trumpeter with whom I made one of my first-ever recordings, *Humming To Myself*, a rarity in that it features Chis on the celeste, one of those instruments like the tuba and the C-melody sax which don't seem to crop up in jazz so much now (well, you never see Courtney Pine using them).

One evening, the Nest boasted a gathering that included Benny Carter, Fats Waller, Coleman Hawkins and half of the great Jimmie Lunceford band, including

Lunceford himself, all drinking and joining in. With such an intimidatingly talented guest list, us regulars stood up to leave the bandstand but Benny said to me,

"No, you stay on".

Anyone who was in the audience that night might remember these jazz giants filling the stage, along with this terrible little white Glasgow face in the middle!

Next thing I knew, I was saying goodbye to Ella and to London because Benny had offered me three months' work in Holland. It was my first proper trip abroad but I didn't get much of a chance to sample the native tongue (if you'll pardon the expression) because everybody there spoke better English than we did. Mind you, there weren't that many Englishmen among us, in fact it's hard to imagine a more cosmopolitan band than that one. Benny had managed to assemble on one stage a combo that included a Cuban, a Welshman, two West Indians and a Scot (guess which one I was).

Holland had a thriving jazz scene then and The Hague was blessed not only by Benny but also - working at a club just down the road from us - Coleman Hawkins, the first major exponent of the tenor saxophone, soon to record his definitive version of *Body And Soul*. The man's ability to project a strongly free and individual jazz style without sacrificing the melody is typified in that classic performance which I'm glad to say is still available today on CD (this chapter's turning into a glorified commercial break; at this rate, I'll soon be extolling the virtues of second-hand Ford Sierras).

Musically, Benny Carter and Coleman Hawkins had a lot in common but they were very different people. Benny was a gentleman while Hawkins was a hooligan! He was another one with a taste for liquid stimulants and I remember the heart-stopping sight of him in Holland, strolling along the quayside wall in a state of severe sozzlement, happily humming jazz tunes and seemingly oblivious of the fact that the wall was easily six feet high but barely four inches wide. It only needed him to put one foot wrong and the world might have lost its leading tenor player about thirty years earlier than it actually did.

Perhaps it was Benny's gentlemanliness that brought the devil out in Hawkins because he couldn't resist a joke at my temporary boss's expense. He used to come and see us play in the afternoon at an open-air seaside venue called the Kursaal (yes, it _was_ summer) and he'd sit there, not opposite the sax section but opposite the brass section. Then after a while, he'd disappear only to return, tenor in hand, and come and sit in with us, not among the saxes but right in the middle of the brass where he'd spend much of his time egging me on to take solos. Benny bore it all with fortitude but he must have felt like a teacher whose class had been invaded by the naughtiest boy in the school.

I cursed my luck around that time because I'd managed to develop a fearfully swollen lip. There I was, about to record with these giants and I was in too much pain even to play a note. It was so bad that they were going to lance it. Then in stepped Dr. Coleman Hawkins who said,

"You come with me, I'll fix it."

He handed me what looked like a half-pint of water. I'd whipped a good third of it down before realising it was vodka! After that, I didn't care what I played.

The Ambrose Octet (spot the guitarist).

Chapter Five

IF IT'S SATURDAY, IT MUST BE AMBROSE

...in which George is hired by a top bandleader, despite his ability to play jazz.

In the immediate pre-war era, for anyone who had trouble telling one day from the next (and with unemployment so high, I don't doubt there were some), help was at hand. All you had to do was put the radio on, wait for what seemed like several weeks for the valves to warm up and tune to the BBC between half past ten and midnight. It had a different dance band on each evening (Lew Stone, Jack Payne, Jack Harris, Jack Jackson, Jack The Ripper etc.) and whichever one you heard would help you to gauge which night it was. If you haven't worked out Ambrose's night yet, try reading the chapter title again, it offers a clue.

Returning to London after three months with Benny Carter in Holland, the next rung on the ladder of my career looked like being unemployment. Then Tommy McQuater the trumpeter (probably my best friend) swung me an audition with the venerable Saturday nighter himself. I say 'swung' but with Ambrose the word was scarcely appropriate and it's a wonder I got taken on. Mentally, I was still in Benny's band, taking solos 15 choruses long, building up ever so gradually to a near frantic pitch by the end. Naturally this involves an understated, economical start: you don't give your all straight away for fear of peaking too soon! But Ambrose wasn't interested in lengthy, original solos and he certainly wasn't au fait with aspects of jazz, his greatest efforts in that direction being the ability to hold a fiddle and count up to four. This was a man of moderate tastes, a lover of Vera Lynn (in the musical sense) because of her simplicity of style and good intonation. What on earth would he make of me? I might be many things but I'm no forces' sweetheart.

When I arrived for the audition, I found he'd stuck down the hardest trombone parts ever, all the Tommy Dorsey solos from things like *Song Of India* and *I'm Getting Sentimental Over You*; dreadfully difficult stuff and while Dorsey himself was the perfect trombonist, I belonged to an entirely different school of playing. For me, the 'Sentimental Gentleman' was <u>too</u> perfect. There was never any doubt that he would deliver a flawless performance but, by the same token, there was never anything surprising to listen out for. I preferred to be on the edge of my seat with a Jack Teagarden effort, thinking 'Is he going to make it? How's he going to do it?' as he kept you wondering till the very last chorus just how successful the solo was going to be. This preference made toying with Dorsey material even harder for me and, having just come out of working in a jazz club, I played the pieces the way I thought they should go. Ambrose then turned to his guitarist Ivor Mairants and I heard him whisper,

"Is that good?"

A fair question, I suppose, since he'd probably never heard them played that way before. Somewhere amid the whisperings, it must have been decided that I would do because in no time I was in a tuxedo, playing *The Lady Is A Tramp* six times a night with a mute on.

Ambrose enjoyed a very up-market image, which could explain why he'd dropped his Christian name of Bert. He was even popular with royalty and if ever there was a function in the ballroom at Buckingham Palace, we used to be engaged, some of us ending up ensconced high in a minstrel's gallery, a location I found myself revisiting about 45 years later (see Chapter 11 - but not now, I haven't written it yet).

Often the nobility would turn up and dance either at the Mayfair or the Cafe de Paris (situated in that same Coventry Street where I used to spin out the brunch at Lyons Corner House). We oscillated between the two venues on a seasonal basis and I think Ambrose had a deal going whereby he would stay at the Mayfair for the duration of the run. Talk about living over the shop!

By this time, Ella and I were living in

West Hampstead, some miles from the shop but an easy enough ride into the West End all the same. The Central London residencies suited me fine and I was happy not to be a regular in The Ambrose Octet which went on tour. The first trombonist, Les Carew, took on that responsibility and the hazardous moments that sometimes went with it. One theatre they played had a drop curtain, as opposed to the tabs that just slither across, and Les had the misfortune to be flexing the slide on his trombone as this heavily-fringed affair began to rise, one of its tassels snatching Les's slide as it went. And there it stayed, in the flies, for the rest of the evening, reducing Les to the role of the world's first silent trombonist. There but for the grace of God, minimal touring and fringeless curtains, went I.

Glancing at the Octet's team photo recently, I was reminded of the presence of one Bert Weedon who later gained fame for his best-selling guitar tutor, *Play In A*

Day. Back then though, he was something of a fish out of water. The rest of the outfit would tease him mercilessly about his solos, asking,

"When are you going to play jazz?"

His standard response was, "I'm saving it."

* * * *

Ambrose was a funny man to work for: he never actually spoke to me for about six months. There was no sinister reason behind this, he just didn't get round to it and I presume he didn't think it was important. Early on, the closest he came to the personal touch was leaning forward to Ivor and asking,

"What's that second trombonist called?"

In time, he went from one extreme to the other and ended up saying I was his right-hand man. Quite why I don't know. I never ran about doing anything for him, but I must have been getting it right somehow because I started being given solos to play. This meant Ambrose had directed the arranger to write in a trombone piece. The only way we had of knowing whether or not he approved of what we'd done was by watching the back of his head. As he always stood facing away from us, it was all we could see. I knew from the slight nod of his bonce that he felt everything was going nicely.

It certainly was for him and I'll admit that being part of his band brought with it a degree of celebrity status. Clearly, the venues we played were among London's most opulent and the weekly broadcast was essential to the band in terms of national profile. Saturday was the big night and, with no Black and White Minstrels to watch on TV for some years yet, the media millions were glued to their wireless sets (some may even have been stapled to them, I forget). I think Ambrose regarded his radio engagement as a necessary evil. He certainly gave that impression to the high-class revellers in the ballroom. On Saturday nights, there was a notice up apologising for the fact that between half past ten and midnight, the band would be a little louder than usual, but hastily reassuring them that after twelve, we'd be back to a muted *Lady Is A Tramp*.

It was fun for us during the broadcast because all the special arrangements would come out, we'd un-mute ourselves and show a little of what we could do. But still people would complain about the noise level. I don't know why. Perhaps they wanted to hear themselves drink their soup.

Mind you, the diners took enough interest in the music to approach the bandstand with requests - good job it wasn't Barrowland (see Chapter 2 - it's all right, I've already written that one). Many a white fiver was crammed into the Ambrosian fist accompanied by a chinless rendering of…

"I say, could you play *The Lady Is A Tramp*?" (this sentence to be read as if it contains no consonants whatsoever). That was such easy money for our leader as most nights we were going to play it next anyway. There may even have been times when folk requested it while it was actually being played. The most we workers saw of these bills was as they made the journey south down Bert's dress trouser pocket. It may seem odd that a major bandleader was allowed to accept gratuities in this way but there was no bye-law saying he couldn't.

Even then, Ambrose had his pride. He gave the shortest of shrifts to one young yahoo who waved a ten shilling note under his nose and asked him to play 'You Are The One'. Mystified, the boss professed not to know it.

"Of course you know it!" insisted the yahoo. "You play it all the time."

He even tried singing it but couldn't

remember the first three words,

"La la la, you are the one..."

Porterphiles among the readership will have spotted already that the missing words were *Night And Day*. Ambrose's response to this was to fish out £4 10s and tell the yahoo to go buy a shirt.

* * * *

I've mentioned the lack of touring enjoyed during my stint with the band, but its popularity did mean the odd trip had to be undertaken. Ambrose was a big hit in Paris so we capitalised on this by sailing across to give the French a none-too-vigorous burst of *La Dame Est Une Trampe*.

Returning home, as we touched down (or since it was by boat, touched along), I mused that our cargo could have been designed as the ultimate test of the detective powers of HM Customs and Excise. Luckily for our clarinettist and saxophonist Billy Amstell, they failed this test with flying reds and greens. He had a consignment of dubious watches as long as his arm...which worked out well because that's where he hid them. At no time was he asked to roll up his sleeve but poor Max Bacon, the drummer, was harbouring a different kind of tick: a nervous one. This manifested itself in the form of what looked like a conspiratorial wink and, if you didn't know him, you'd swear he was letting you in on some grand piece of mischief.

Not surprisingly, the customs men didn't know him and when he accompanied his 'nothing to declare' statement with a good half-dozen winks of the eye, they knew they'd got their man. There and then, on the quayside, they thoroughly searched him, his luggage and even his drum-kit in the certain knowledge that he was concealing some red hot contraband...which he wasn't. Meanwhile, Billy looked on with a 'butter wouldn't melt in my embouchere' expression, knowing full well that, if asked, he could tell them the time in six continents.

The Squads at the trough and in the field of 'conflict'.

Chapter Six
ODDS AND SQUADS

...in which war hero Chisholm keeps the home fires burning with some hot jazz.

War broke out in the Mayfair Hotel. That's not to say that those genteel diners for whom Ambrose always played 'too loudly' on a Saturday night suddenly started hurling bread rolls and table napkins at us, nor was it a throwback to my Glasgow ballroom days where the best form of sanctuary from violence was to be found under the piano (besides, I'd switched to trombone and you try sliding under one of them).

What I mean is, we were playing at the Mayfair when Neville Chamberlain, the only man ever to get a round of applause just by holding up a piece of paper (even origami experts have to fiddle about with it first), announced the outbreak of hostilities. As it turned out, they were to be a long time in coming, but we didn't know that then so six of us Ambrosians did the decent thing and volunteered for the Air Force. Now before going any further, I really ought to stress that this seemingly highly patriotic act was in no way connected with bravery. It simply occurred to us that if we joined up early, we might get the chance to play.

The Magnificent Six were first but not least, myself, Tommy McQuater and Archie Craig on trumpets, Harry Lewis on reeds (clarinet and alto sax), the pianist and singer Jimmy Miller and Sid Colin the singing guitarist, later to become an honest broker of jokes, japes and wheezes in the noble profession of comedy scriptwriting (notably for *The Army Game, Carry On Spying* and *Up Pompeii!*). So there we were: six characters in search of an orchestra.

Proper bona fide war memoirs always seem to find their heroes stationed at some thrilling overseas location like Anzio or Tobruk. We got posted to Uxbridge. Still, as parts of Middlesex go, it was pretty damn thrilling! Uxbridge was our parent station but for most other people it seemed to be a place you stayed at for a couple of weeks before being sent somewhere else. It was the perfect setting for us because we got ourselves attached to the

Central Band of the RAF, conveniently also stationed there.

Because there were only six of us, we had to try and build ourselves up. So any time a trumpeter or a saxophonist found themselves in Uxbridge prior to posting, we'd ask if we could keep them there. We carried on collecting stray musicians in this way till we'd amassed a personnel of fourteen. On top of this, the Central Band also had a highly impressive roll call of names from the classical world including Maurice Westerby, Freddie Grinky and David Martin in the string section along with horn players like Norman Del Mar and Dennis Brain.

Money couldn't have bought the orchestra that a war brought together but these boys were wasted in the Central Band because their conductor, Wing Commander O'Donnell, had until then been in charge of a military outfit, playing what can only be described as yatatatata-ta music. O'Donnell came to be known locally as 'Two Gun

Rudy' on account of his sideways-on stance on the podium, looking as though he was sporting a couple of revolvers. This seemed appropriate enough since the musicians under him must have felt like they were at gunpoint. He had Dennis Brain and Del Mar and all these great string players knocking out this terrible, hackneyed old stuff and saluting in 4/4 time as though they were performing at the Edinburgh Military Tattoo. I still have trouble remaining vertical and not collapsing with hysterical laughter whenever I see a band doing that.

Brain was very young then, liked a few pints and was an absolute genius of a horn player. Understandably he used to get very bored with what he was being given to do. All those guys should have been playing Elgar and Bach and Mozart, except I'm not sure Two Gun Rudy knew how any of them went. Occasionally Dennis would tunnel his way out under the music stand and emerge where we were rehearsing in the gents' ablutions - beautiful acoustics in there, it was nice to get a breath of fresh air. He liked the way we were playing and it soon came about that I was writing jazz choruses for him to perform on the French horn, which he did brilliantly. He used to love that, especially after a non-stop diet of yatatatata tat.

We'd taken to calling ourselves The Squadronaires - unofficially. The Air Council forbade the unqualified use of this commercial sounding name. I can just picture some red-faced, handlebar-moustach-ed Air Vice-Marshal recoiling with a cry of 'Ugh! Smacks of trade!' - so on best behaviour days, we were billed as 'The Royal Air Force Dance Orchestra (by permission of the Air Council)'; a snappy little title, you'll agree. By way of a minor concession, in very, very small letters underneath, it said 'The Squadronaires'. But whenever we got out of town, we were 'The Squadronaires' in big letters and all the other rubbish at the bottom.

With an eye to the future, we reasoned that if we lasted the war out and went commercial afterwards (further bouts of re-coiling from red-faced Air Marshal), we'd need to construct a scale of charges for arrangements. When finalised, the tariff read thus:-

Concert arrangement a la Paul Whiteman: 3s. Od.

Straightforward jazz or commercial chart: 2s. Od.

What a bargain!

This compensated for the fact that the arrangers were tied down orchestrating while the others were out on the equally important assignment of boozing. However, I managed to devise a method whereby I could orchestrate and booze at the same time: it was called having two hands. Eric Breeze and I used to do unison trombone solos as a feature - the only two-man solos in the biz - but I had the benefit of knowing what was coming up because I'd written it. Eric, on the other hand, was having to read and play from sight in my phrasing! Tremendously difficult to do but he did it to perfection every time. I had enormous respect for Eric.

The co-operative status of the Squads was inspired by the way the Bob Crosby band was run and our style was based roughly on their Dixieland sound, only we were bigger. The influence of American orchestras on the British scene was very strong at the time, with the swing era at its peak. In fact, there used to be this great wall of demarcation between US and British musicians in terms of quality but I'm glad to say it no longer exists: now we've got players who are every bit as good as theirs.

America's entry into the war allowed us to experience a lot of their musicians at first hand. Not surprisingly, the Service Orchestra under Major Glenn Miller (he insisted on the 'Major') tended to dominate the forces entertainment scene, certainly in the latter days of the war, but I and most of my mates never considered them to be the best. Instead, we all voted for the US Navy Band under Sam Donahue, the band that had come almost lock, stock and barrel out of the Artie Shaw Service Band. To our ears, they sounded far more exciting and they outswung the Miller boys every time.

One occasion found us playing at an American soldiers' hostel in Piccadilly. It was a special show for US forces and it had representative bands from all sorts: George Melachrino and the British Expeditionary Forces, Robert Farnon and the Canadian Band, Glenn Miller and the band of the American Air Force as well as the Donahue clan which included a trombonist formerly with Benny Goodman called Dick Lefevre. They wanted us there for rehearsal at the ungodly time of 10 a.m. (does anything actually happen at that hour?) and Dick must have sensed a certain fragility about me because he asked if I'd had breakfast. The answer, predictably, was no so he said,

"Would you like to share my breakfast?"

Well, it would have been churlish to refuse, wouldn't it? So we went round the back of the building and from his instrument case he produced a bottle of whisky. We shared his breakfast all right!

The atmosphere in the Donahue band was far less militaristic than others. All right so it was wartime, but why this assumption that you had to be of a certain rank in order to wave a stick? By all accounts, the Miller band was run along pretty regimented lines even in peacetime so maybe they didn't notice much difference. Often a scapegoat principle operated where one member (usually the drummer) became the butt of every barb. In the case of the Miller band, the drummer was Sergeant Ray McKinley whose function it was to keep order. The thinking behind this seemed to be that you can only control a bunch of musicians if you've got three stripes on your arm. We suffered from this mentality as well to the extent that Tommy

McQuater was made a corporal and Jimmy Miller became a sergeant, presumably on the grounds that Jimmy was out front, therefore he must be leadership material. Once - but only once - we made the mistake of introducing the term 'Musicians' Union' when addressing a regular. It was met with the response,

"What do you mean, union? There's a bloody war on!"

From the point of view of active military service, we had a quiet war. We were neither fish, fowl nor anything else beginning with f (though some may disagree). Every time we appeared at Uxbridge, we were decked out in things they had in the stores but wouldn't issue us with, like monkey jackets. So we'd be wearing cut-price versions, not with brass buttons but the bakelite equivalent that didn't need polishing, usually provoking cries from our superiors of "Where did you get these?!" and "Look at the length of that hair!", swiftly followed by sotto voce instructions to "Post them, for God's sake!" - and that was us, away as soon as we arrived, off to somewhere in France usually. We did Europe but we never got out to the Far East. Mind you, we did get to the North-East.

There was a balloon centre station near Newcastle called Longbenton (a good comedy name for starters) which played host to our happy band. As ever, we arrived in style aboard an open-topped truck of the crash-bang-wallop variety. Even now it's a fair drive to Newcastle, but then it was all A-roads so we didn't get there till about three in the morning. Naturally, it was pouring with rain, and even more naturally, there was no one on the sentry gate, but we did see an airman coming towards us. We told him we were the band. He didn't know anything about a band. We asked him, where do we sleep? He pointed to a hut in the distance and suggested we try that. We did. The hut was empty but for various mattresses, all of them wringing wet due to the open-plan roof (a chorus of *Hearts and Flowers* can be heard in the background as

80

Chisholm goes for the sympathy vote). Actually, it wasn't too bad because we'd consumed enough liquor for it not to matter that much. Only when we were all bedded down for the night and the hut was alive with snores did it occur to one of us that some lunatic would be bound to come round about 5 a.m. and kick hell out of the door as part of a "wakey wakey" routine. So preventive measures were taken...as indeed was the light-bulb, right out of its socket.

Sure enough, around two hours later, along comes the Station Warrant Officer, an archetypal 'regular', complete with the regulation cropped hair, neanderthal forehead and boils on the back of the neck. He launched into the set routine from which these guys would never deviate, kicked open the door, flicked the light switch and barked,

"Wakey wakey, feet on the floor, you bunch of..." (you can imagine the rest).

Then came a voice from the back in the dark inviting him to push off (or words to that effect), and this bloke was astounded. Nobody had ever spoken to him like that before.

"Who said that?", he demanded and I think it was Tommy McQuater who replied,

"Joe Stalin"

"Ah yes", he said, "but what's your number?"

At that point, he must have paused to wonder why the light hadn't gone on. Maybe his brain-cell got as far as deducing that the bulb must have gone. Maybe he thought to himself, 'What if they're a bunch of officers on a top secret mission or something?', because after that, he never came near the hut again. We would safely retire there, a bit wet perhaps, but secure in the knowledge that we could sleep till whatever time we liked without being discovered. Oh, the luxury of a lie-in in wartime!

Station Warrant Officers weren't

known for their towering degrees of intelligence. Some of them found it hard to spell IQ, let alone have one. At Uxbridge, we posed a pronunciation problem for our man because a lot of the names were Italian, Jewish or Scottish. Undaunted, he'd begin by shouting,

"Schrieber...Tilt...Koblentz...Copperman...Bogam...Boga...Bog..dismiss!"

It's a shame he never got as far as me, I'm sure even he could have managed Chisholm.

* * * *

Our awayday gigs would often involve staying in pubs - a hardship, I know, but somehow we struggled through. When we played Hartlepool, the venue was quite a long way from our licensed digs and on returning at about two in the morning, I discovered that I'd left the key to my room in a very safe place - inside the room. There wasn't an outdoor key and obviously no one was still up at that hour so I looked at the brickwork and saw there were a few little niches I might be able to use as stepping stones up to the toilet window which was just about big enough to get through. It was a daunting prospect but I decided to give it a try because showbiz is all about struggling to reach the top without going down the pan. My incentive was increased by the fact that it had just started raining, so I climbed up with great difficulty and I'd just got one leg over the window sill when I heard a voice from the ground reciting that familiar catch-phrase of

"Hallo Hallo Hallo!".

Pausing only to think 'Oh God!', I looked down at the rather stout, tomato-faced, uniformed figure standing with his hands behind his back.

"What are we up to, then?"

'We' is obviously a term misused by Queens and constables alike. 'We' weren't up to anything, at least <u>he</u> wasn't. I, on the other hand, was up to the apex of my trousers in window ledge, one leg home and dry (no mean feat considering its proximity to the toilet basin) while the other dangled recklessly in the night. Not the ideal position from which to deliver a detailed explanation of my behaviour, but my mammy had brought me up to be polite and always answer policemen when they ask you what the hell you're doing, so I said,

"I've left my key inside and I..."

"Why are you out here so late?"

"Ah, well I'm in a band, you see, and I…"

"A band? What's a band?"

"You know, an orchestra. I'm with The Squadronaires."

"Squadronaires? What do you play?"

"The trombone."

"Shame it weren't the trumpet. I've got a recording of that Nat Gonella playing the trumpet."

My thoughts were along the lines of 'For God's sake, get on with it!' but I heard myself say,

"Oh really?"

"Aye. Do you know a tune called *Troublesome Trumpet*?"

A moment ago, he didn't even know what a band was. Now he's throwing Gonella titles at me.

"Er, no I'm afraid not. That's a trumpet piece, not trombone." I was beginning to giggle by now.

"Oh I've got Nat Gonella playing it. Plays it grand. Lovely, really lovely."

There was a long pause. Then,

"Goodnight."

And he left me there, straddling! No offer of help, nothing. If only Nat Gonella had played the trombone!

* * * *

Our penchant for staying in pubs continued when we did a week-long stint in Liverpool, but we thought it'd be good to find a nice, quiet little pub where nobody bothers you. Sure enough, we alighted on this tiny place with just the one room and only one bloke behind the bar, cleaning glasses. All fourteen of us descended on him like a bunch of locusts, but ones with a taste for something a little stronger than vegetation. He couldn't pull the pints fast enough, to say nothing of the whisky chasers. So there was a whole week of that and then we left and didn't go back to Liverpool for about another four months. When we did return, we eagerly made our way back to that same quiet little pub only to find a different guy cleaning glasses behind the counter.

"What happened to old Fred?" we asked (not all fourteen of us at once, you understand).

"Oh it's funny about him", the new man replied. "It must have been three or four months ago. The takings suddenly shot up, then after a week, they shot down again. And the brewery thought he was fiddling the till so they gave him the bullet."

The poor sod had lost his job all on account of thirsty Squadronaires!

* * * *

Some jobs took us further afield and I still have a make-shift diary, scribbled on a pad of ruled 'Bloc Correspondence Marathon' paper which captures the atmosphere (and anticipation) of an overseas posting in 1944. After recording a series of innoculations that left me more perforated than the average teabag, it went on:-

Friday 17th November

Left Uxbridge. Arrived at Vine Street station, hung around for a couple of hours and finally got the train to Paddington. Had to shift about two hundred kit-bags between us (other people's) and all our stuff and instruments. Some officers travelling with us tried to make us lift their stuff and were refused! Finally got on trucks and arrived at

Fenchurch Street station, passing down Edgware Road in the process. Same business with kit-bags and instruments, plus the officers' efforts to make us move their stuff. They were still unlucky! Boarded the train and arrived at Purfleet, near Tilbury Docks, where we found we wouldn't travel that night, so we were taken by truck, but not before the officers had another go at us and were told politely but firmly to "---- off!", to Purfleet transit camp, the mud heap of Britain! On our arrival there, amidst mud and rain, at about five o'clock, we were greeted with no civility and about four V2s in twenty minutes. Very naughty! We were eventually led, or rather we struggled through the mud, to a tent which was swimming in water. We then had to draw blankets and fill some palliases (a sort of mattress) with new straw to lie on. I felt very low that night but got over it as everybody was in the same boat. Couldn't sleep for V2s bursting every ten minutes.

Saturday 18th

Woke up fully expecting to move off, but went through all the same routine of rain, mud and naafi beer. Did a show for the boys at night which went down very well. Went to bed accompanied by....V2s!!!

Tuesday 21st

Can't believe it: we're moving off!! Left Purfleet and boarded the L.S.T. (Landing Ship, Tanks), all set to go. We moved off and...anchored off Southend pier! Were told we wouldn't sail that night so gave a show for the crew and lads on board. The crew were wonderful guys and real hard workers. Went to bed. Couldn't sleep for intense cold.

Thursday 23rd

Sailed at 3.30 a.m. Woken around 8 o'clock by some lousy sergeant who told me to start getting the place cleaned out. Ha ha! There was Billy Nicholls and I with sweeping brushes and floor mops, cleaning out the 'cabin' and washing down the walls. Usual routine until arrival at Ostende at 4 p.m., then by truck to Blankenburghe (Brussels) where we were billeted for the night, which was free. Investigated the town and went to bed.

Saturday 25th

Travelled to Brussels and everything looked much brighter as there was an officer we knew there who was partly in charge of us. Played at the Malcolm Club for a dance.

Sunday 26th

Free day! Looked Brussels over, had a few <u>very</u> weak cognacs, were stopped by countless old men with cards for admittance to brothels. Finally to bed.

Monday 27th

Travelled to Toumain (France) and played a show at Forgennes, just outside. Got to bed (on the floor).

Tuesday 28th

Proceeded to Genech and played at the chateau there. Can't remember much about this. Got to bed on the floor again.

Wednesday 29th

To a hospital voluntarily and played to wounded in the afternoon, then further on to do a show for an R.A.F. station.

Thursday 30th

Proceeded 200 miles to Eindhoven in Holland via Brussels, Mons and Allemanches. On arrival, found that people were starving and gave away all our sandwiches to kids and grown-ups. Pitiful state of affairs. Played at the Malcolm Club where nobody knew anything about us until we were finished. Slept in the first decent bed since we started.

Sunday 3rd December

Were instructed to move to Antwerp (Belgium) to play a show. Journey of 180 miles. On arrival there, found they had moved to another station 50 miles back from where we'd come, finally arrived there in the worst rainstorm ever, but too late to do a show.

Nice reception here in spite of our failure to arrive on time. Pretty good beds too!

Monday 4th

Proceeded to Breda in Holland and played show. Bought Earle's first present here.

Tuesday 5th

Played show outside Breda near Tilbury. Met marvellous Typhoon pilots and got a bit high on scotch and English beer. A <u>very</u> rare treat. Back on the floor again.

Thursday 7th

Moved to Halle where we played a show, the audience consisting of mostly Belgian people. Were informed that four Russian officers were also present. After the show, went to the bar and sorted the Russian guys out. Had a marvellous night with them. Great experience. One was a political commissar! Went to bed on the good old floor again.

Friday 8th

Moved to Ghent where we were lumbered with the corniest acts yet ever seen on <u>any</u> stage!!! Cold floor a blessed relief.

Saturday 9th

Travelled to Brussels. Sent to wrong station again and just made the show. Bloody cold in hangar where the show was held. Big row about our being messed around. We won!

Sunday 10th

Played big charity show at the ENSA Garrison Theatre (very beautiful theatre) in front of Lord and Lady Cunningham. Big success. Back to barracks to sleep on bed (yes, Bed!!)

Tuesday 12th

Returned voluntarily to place where we missed the show before, did two to make up for our lack of shows here previously. Very well received and Frank Engelman brought the BBC van up. We recorded part of the show from here. Bought presents today.

Wednesday 13th

Residents Palace Officers Clubs. Played show. Very stiff 'do', had another go at London. Met the alleged Wing-Commander in charge of Air Movements and 'confirmed' our departure by air for the following day.

Thursday 14th

Due to leave Belgium by air and be in England by lunch time, but fog prevented this and we had to return to barracks, Brussels.

Friday 15th

Reported this morning at the airport and, after various promises, ended up at 6.30 in the evening still not departed. Waited around for mail plane leaving at eight but it didn't go. Hoping against hope to leave Belgium tomorrow as we've been told to come back Sat. morning for this same mail plane. Back to barracks where I started writing this diary.

Saturday 16th

Reported to aerodrome again and got pushed around by high-ranking officers getting in first. Sat around and were finally told to go by sea. We rushed by truck to Ostende where an Air Sea Rescue launch awaited us. Loaded all stuff on, then captain told us to take it off again as he wasn't sailing that day!! Were taken to Blankenburghe where we slept.

Sunday 17th

Got up early and reported to the embarkation office where the officer told us there was nothing at all today. All went to the films and, on coming out, were told that a boat had been and left and they couldn't find us!!! Luckily enough the boat developed boiler trouble and didn't leave. That was one disappointment we missed.

Monday 18th

At last!!! Got down to Ostende and eventually got on board ship. Met Joe Loss and boys on same ship. Could have been home tonight but ship anchored off Folkestone to catch the tide into harbour. Disembarked at midnight and were put into billets.

Tuesday 19th

Set off by train at 6.40 a.m. and finally arrived in London. The whole tour was a shocking farce as far as organisation was concerned.

Those pages require one or two footnotes of explanation. To anyone young and lucky enough not to know the horror of the V2, I should point out that, unlike the doodlebug, it had a charming little habit of dropping on you without any prior warning, no whistling noise as it fell from the sky, nothing. The explosion itself was the first you knew about it. Sneaky, huh? I mean even the VAT inspector tells you when he's going to call.

The reference to a first present for

Earle (Monday 4th December) reminds me that by this time Ella and I had a new-born son, our first and only child together. In later years, Earle was to prove a very resourceful young man, opening a hairdressing salon with a friend in Florida and eventually taking it over as his own concern. Currently, he's a mortgage banker (am I in the wrong business?).

Our drinking session with the Russians may not seem quite so remarkable these days, now that it's quite possible to get smashed with a few comrades and all end up singing 'I Belong To G1asnost', but then our Western eyes saw the Soviets as an extremely dour bunch, not at all prone to high jinks. Happily, the political commissar and his chums confounded our preconceptions.

Clearly I had a fair command of the English language in 1944, describing that doyen of Reithian broadcasters Franklyn Engelman as having "brought the BBC van up" as if he were same kind of lorry driver!

* * * *

1945 was significant for two events: the war ended and the Squadronaires didn't. As soon as we were demobbed (I still wear the suit), we were able to turn the band into the successful venture we'd envisaged at Uxbridge without having to worry about any outbreaks of apoplexy from red-faced Air Vice-Marshals. We continued to appear in uniform and the RAF couldn't really object to that, especially as we did umpteen concerts whose proceeds went to the British Legion or the RAF Benevolent Fund, a matter of literally thousands of pounds. There's one little gripe I have about that. After the war, I was skint myself with a wife and baby to support on 7/6 a day and when I applied to these two organisations to help me out, they wouldn't loan me a penny.

"Oh no, it's not wartime now" was the somewhat irrelevant explanation. What were we supposed to do, sleep in the street? I found myself resorting to the line,

"Do you realise I'm a Squadronaire?"

Sounds so shallow on reflection, doesn't it?

"What did you do in the war, daddy?"

"I was a Squadronaire!"

The Squads on stage: Jock Cummings (drums), Arthur Maiden (bass), GC, Sgt. Jimmy Miller (leader) and Sid Colin.

Chapter Seven
THE MAN FROM AUNTIE

...in which CC cops a chunk of the licence fee for backing the Guv'nor and the Goons.

My demob from The Squadronaires finally occurred in the early 1950s, more than half a decade after the end of the war that had brought us all together in the first place - nice to know we were that much more popular than the fighting.

With very little breathing space in between, my RAF music career was succeeded by one in another of our great military institutions, the BBC. Their Show Band - the equivalent of today's Radio Big Band - had a large string section: eight brass, five saxes, and four rhythm plus the Cliff Adams Singers and a series of celebrity comperes including Rikki Fulton, later to achieve TV cult status as the lugubrious Reverend I.M. Jolly, and Stan Stennett to whom I'll return shortly.

At that time, radio was king. Well, to be strictly accurate, George VI was king - but radio came a pretty close second. TV was still in its infancy, not only resembling a goldfish bowl in size and shape but often in content as well: the fish swimming in the tank, the potter's wheel, the kitten playing with a ball of wool, the four-minute London to Brighton train journey, the kitten playing with the fish...no wonder radio was king.

This was borne out by the fact that visiting American artistes of the calibre of Frank Sinatra were more attracted to sound studios than to ones with cameras in them. Not only did Francis Albert show up to record with us but he brought with him a selection of Nelson Riddle arrangements which were more than a joy to play, especially his glorious interpretation of the old number, *Birth Of The Blues*. The glee with which we embraced such an enormous musical opportunity was inevitably tinged with a nagging fear along the lines of 'What if he doesn't like us?'. Sinatra was not known for suffering fools (usually it was the fools who suffered) and it did emerge that he had harboured misgivings about the ability of a BBC house orchestra to cope with the Riddle repertoire. But he took to us and became very complimentary, especially towards the brass section among whom he had decided to stand. This breach of microphone protocol brought the sound engineer scurrying from his box in an attempt to persuade the great man back to his own designated area. But in the manner of the song that Paul Anka hadn't yet written for him, Sinatra did it his way. He was very reasonable about it. He simply told the engineer,

"Either I do it like this or I don't do it at all!"

Our studio manager, correctly surmising that this didn't offer a great deal of leeway for negotiation, then pondered his next problem: how the hell was he going to record it? Surrounded by trumpets and trombones, the vocalist was unlikely to be heard to his best advantage (or even at all!) but, proving the validity of an old cliché involving necessity, invention and motherhood, the engineer not only arranged matters so that Sinatra was audible but in the process he achieved what turned out to be one of the best balances on any BBC recording of that time. Maybe the singer should have stood among the brass more often.

* * * *

Luckily, my Corporation days didn't confine me to the studio. Recording sessions can be tremendous fun but they don't compare with the atmosphere on a live audience show, so I was very glad to be one of the musicians providing anarchic accompaniment to the antics of The Goons. The orchestra was conducted by a man called Wally Stott who later became a woman called Angela Morley, which goes to prove that times change but not as much as people.

Of course, the music was incidental to the spoken comedy but an affinity developed between Spike Milligan and myself. He seemed to like the way I larked about on the trombone and when he organised the recording session for *The Ying Tong Song* and *I'm Walking Backwards For*

Christmas, I was booked in at EMI along with a rhythm section, a small string section and an incongruous-looking operatic soprano. If it had been anyone other than Spike in charge, I'd have thought I was in the wrong room - but he had plans for the poor prima donna. When it came to her big moment with the string section, the engineer, understandably, put a microphone in front of her face. Immediately, Spike told him to adjust it so that it pointed straight at her stomach. This accounts for the bizarre three-times-removed quality she achieved when singing *Take Me Back To Vienna* amidst all the yingtongiddilipoes.

As well as exploring the comic possibilities of the trombone in the series, I was singled out for a number of speaking parts. The first, in 1956, was in a Caledonian epic entitled *The MacReekie Rising of '74* in which I appeared as Chisholm MacChisholm the Steaming Kilt, threatening to wreak revenge on the sassenachs for abducting our clan's hairy caber. Going against the advice of Major Dennis Bloodnok, military coward and Bart., Seagoon refuses to return the item and war breaks out with the Scots hordes firing porridge and the English retaliating with Brown Windsor soup. Even more sensibly, I cropped up later in the same run in the episode *Wings Over Dagenham* as 'a dour Scots gentleman in a grease-stained body', helping Neddy build the world's first hairyplane (we were all a lot hairier in those days) and almost exactly one year on, I dusted off the Caledonian twang to assist Inspector Seagoon in investigating *The Great String Robberies*, my voice emerging from under a navy red kilt. My character boasted of ventriloquial powers ("I throw ma voice: sometimes through ma knees, sometimes through ma shins and some-times up a ma nose").

The first two of these editions were co-written by Spike and the late Larry Stephens but Goon archivists may recall that *MacReekie* was not just peculiar for my presence but also for Spike's absence. The phenomenal strain of writing the shows occasionally left him too unwell to perform in them. He's on record as saying the series cost him his sanity, but those of us who didn't have the burden of hammering out a fresh script every week were more able to enjoy the inspired lunacy that made the show unique.

I warmed to all three stars as much as anything because of their musical leanings. Peter Sellers was a frustrated drummer and wouldn't leave the timpani alone during rehearsals; Harry was always breaking into cod operatic arias which he was more than able to sing properly and Milligan was a fair jazz trumpeter, unless he thought the audience was against him, in which case he had been known to throw the instrument down and storm off with a cry of,

"You hate me, don't you?!"

Not that Spike didn't derive enormous pleasure from carrying Goonish behaviour over into real life. Many of the programmes were recorded at the Camden Theatre in North London, not far from a firm of funeral directors. One day, Spike went in there with Harry in tow, the pair of them lay flat on the floor and Spike called out,

"Shop!"

Secombe was out the door the minute the undertaker arrived but Milligan had to see the joke through to its natural end, trying to get himself measured up for a coffin. I'm amazed he didn't go the whole hog and insist on being buried.

Satchmo and GC the wrong side of a mosquito net.

Chapter Eight

SATCHMO ON THE SOUTH BANK

...in which George goes from Ella to Etta and learns from Louis on laxatives.

My marriage to Ella survived the war, but not the peace. It goes without saying that a broken relationship is painful and tragic and really shakes up those concerned, especially when any kids are involved - but there, I've said it anyway.

In this case, the situation was complicated further by the fact that I had fallen in love with the wife of a trumpeter I'd been working with, and it was mutual. Her name, almost coincidentally, was Etta.

The difficulties presented by all this can be imagined but as much as these things ever can, it all came right in the end. I had left West Hampstead and set up home with Etta. We married just as soon as the old-style, slow-moving divorce laws would allow and had two children, both of whom have grown up taking an active interest in music (without any undue pressure being exerted by their old man). My daughter Carole is a great Billie Holiday fan and has a fine singing voice herself. In recent years, she's appeared at gigs with the

Gentlemen of Jazz (whoever they are) and we've also made a record together. Garry, my son, is a keen lyric-writer and I recorded some of his work with, of all things, Hendon Brass Band - a superb ensemble.

But to return to the 50s, perhaps it was the failure of my first marriage that prompted me to rethink my approach to work. I'd almost lived more out of a suitcase than I had with Ella, what with the war and one-night stands at far corners of the country. It gets a bit embarrassing when you have to be introduced to your own wife, and when she tells you what the kiddie did today and you weren't there, you begin to realise you're in danger of missing your children grow up. That's what made me leave the Squadronaires in the first place. As a freelance musician, I could be a little more choosy about live dates. By and large, I would tend to take work in London and only venture outside when I could be sure of getting back the same night. In terms of jazz, this narrowed the field but we didn't starve, thanks to my BBC Show

Band residency, and anyway the calibre of the one-off gigs could be pretty high, particularly when they involved meeting and working with an old hero.

In 1956, a relief fund was set up in response to the fact that the Russians had dropped in unexpectedly on their Hungarian neighbours, leaving them a little short of supplies. One of Britain's efforts in this direction was to hold a benefit concert at the still relatively new Royal Festival Hall on London's South Bank and the chosen conductor had, in a previous incarnation, been among the classical horn players I'd encountered during the war at Uxbridge. He was asked to put in an orchestra, so he booked the formidable London Symphony along with a smaller jazz group including the drummer Jack Parnell, Sid Phillips on clarinet, Lennie Bush on bass and I was asked to bring my trombone, the idea being to recreate up to a point the sort of thing Paul Whiteman had been doing in the 20s. Flying over from the States to join us (at his own expense) was the focal point of the whole evening, Louis Armstrong.

Imagine my excitement. I don't have to, I can remember it! As a young shaver (or in the case of my upper lip, non-shaver), I used to play along to Armstrong solos as they scratched away at me on the old wind-up gramophone in Glasgow, pretending we were on stage together - and now...! The prospect of working with the great 'Satchelmouth' (which had long-since been shortened to Satchmo) was some sort of pinnacle for me, as it was for everyone there...with the possible exception of the conductor.

Prior to coming over, Louis had recorded the *Porgy and Bess* suite alongside Ella Fitzgerald and he decided to bring some of the parts with him to perform at this concert. It was all highly impressive stuff with the LSO there and our little jazz group coming out of the middle to play then merging back in again. All went well until it came to the part where Louis was meant to sing,

"Nobody knows the trouble I've seen,

Nobody knows but Jesus"

when it became obvious to the audience that the orchestra and the soloist were at variance and the boat was rocking slightly! Rather than follow the artist as he should have done, the conductor had decided he was going to do it his way. This consisted of a somewhat staccato approach to Mr George Gershwin's music, as opposed to the laid-back, rolling feel that Louis was trying to achieve. By this time, the only things rolling were Louis' eyes. To make his point, he chose to sing,

"Nobody knows the trouble I've seen,

Nobody knows but... JESUS! !"

The emphasis on the last word and the fact that it was intended as a comment on the orchestration was not lost on the conductor who, professional to the last, threw down his baton and stomped off the podium. But the whole place lit up at this; after all, they'd only really come to see Louis.

We should have guessed there was going to be friction from the way things had been developing at rehearsal. Suffering from an advanced case of twisted knickers, our stick-waving pal was circling Louis, insisting,

"I must know where to bring the orchestra in after you come out for - what is it? - 'When The Saints Go Traipsing In'. I must know how many bars…it's a big orchestra."

Louis tried to reassure him.

"Man, we're going to have a ball!"

To which the conductor replied,

"How terribly singular."

* * * *

Louis Armstrong was exactly as I'd ex-

expected and hoped him to be: a man who really enjoyed life and wouldn't let anything worry him. Just as well, really, for our conductor's sake. If that had been someone with the temperament of, say, Miles Davis, I imagine the conductor would still be undergoing surgery to have a trumpet removed.

We were all in awe of Louis and I remember going up to him afterwards and saying,

"I've never asked anyone for a picture but I must have one of you."

He wasn't sure if he had any with him but, after rummaging through his briefcase, he announced,

"I've got this one but don't show your wife!"

It was a 12 x 10 of him sitting on the lavatory seat, a great expanse of posterior flesh contrasting with the line of his jock strap, a hair net on his head and a packet in his hand bearing the legend, 'Swiss Kriss'.

It was the trade name of a kind of laxative pretzel which he was being paid to endorse.

Above the title was a likeness of some comely brunette in a low-cut blouse whose presence there was puzzling: she didn't look like she suffered from con-stipation. Clearly, Louis was convinced of the product's healing powers because, as he handed me the photo, he said,

"Man, you gotta leave it all behind!"

GC with his famous collection of microphones.

Chapter Nine

BLACK AND WHITE TELEVISION

...in which the face of Chisholm has 405 lines on it.

Meanwhile, back at the Beeb, my time with the Show Band came to an end, as did the 1950s, as did the Goons. By the time their final episode (*The Last Smoking Seagoon*) went out in early 1960, Peter Sellers was big in films, Harry was big in musicals (and round the waist) and Spike was not far off co-writing and starring in his oddest work of all, *The Bed-Sitting Room*, of which I fear there'll be more later.

Apart from the massive amount of fun I'd had on that show, it had greatly helped me develop the comedic side of my nature as a performer, which was a stroke of luck because in my next job I was going to need it. Earlier, I mentioned Stan Stennett whom I'd met in his Show Band compere days. He was also involved in *The Black And White Minstrel Show* which at that time featured instrumental interludes from Norrie Paramor and the Big Ben Banjo Band. When Norrie's contract came to an end, Stan suggested to the producer George Inns that he should give me a shot. So when George rang and asked if I'd like to do one, I decided that if I went on and did the usual Dixieland spot with a small group, it'd probably be met by an overwhelming chorus of 'Mmm, very nice, next please'. Instead, I resolved to jolly it up and, perhaps because of this, got invited back on a regular basis. But there was no fixed length to my spot in the show. Every week, I used to go to George Inns and ask,

"How long have I got?"

and he'd say,

"Girls, how long does it take to change from the blue into the pink? About a minute and a half? Okay George, you've got a minute and a half."

Trying to put together a worthwhile piece of nonsense proved to be hard work, especially as its duration was dictated by how long it took the Television Toppers to swap frocks. What can you do in ninety seconds? Usually, I'd try and dig up some pseudo-comic slowish piece for the middle section, but that meant whatever went either side of it had to go like the clappers otherwise I'd never fit it in. But then again, it was a solo spot in front of a massive Saturday night audience during the first wave of the television boom (by then, the kitten had just about finished playing with the fish).

Working to a camera was a whole new discipline for me and, in some ways, a terrifying one. The autocue machine was not yet in service and neither was my ability to learn lines. I used to marvel at performers who could get whole sentences off pat, much less full speeches. Of course, there were idiot boards but alas, there were also idiots. More than once, the boards were held up in the wrong order, which would lead people into saying the likes of 'Good evening, ladies and gentlemen and…I hope you'll join us again next week when we'll…welcome to tonight's show…be back'.

As a newcomer to the medium, I was astounded by its illusory quality. The

Minstrel show was transmitted from the Television Theatre (formerly and latterly the Shepherds Bush Empire) and despite the large number of artists involved, they were always heavily outnumbered on the studio floor by technicians and technology. There was a sensation of being hemmed in on all sides by great lumps of mechanical hardware, but George Inns' camera direction would have the viewer believe we were playing in an area the size of the Grand Canyon. How in the name of Cecil B. DeMille did he do it?

Seeing yourself on the screen for the first time is agony. My God, do I really look like that? Can you believe those over-the-top gestures?! It taught me a lot about scaling my act down and relying on the most minimal of actions and expressions. Also, there was an aura of danger about the whole thing which enhanced it for me. Poor George would never know precisely what I'd be doing until show time - and as it was a live show, that didn't give him much power of intervention. So the responsibility for what went out in those however many half-minutes was mine and, although the comedy was a subsidiary part of the show, it did build up a following of its own which was sustained when the whole Minstrel package took up residence in the Victoria Palace Theatre.

Along with Stan Stennett and self, there was the young Leslie Crowther (with whom I appeared on the Minstrel TV show as well as on *Crackerjack*) and a very fine comedienne called Margo Henderson. Our predecessors in the Victoria Palace were The Crazy Gang and severe doubts were harboured as to whether the home-grown Minstrel show could hold its own after an act like that. It was three-and-a-half years later when I left the company and the show continued to thrive long after. Not only did everyone know The Black And White Minstrels but the principal singers were becoming household names too, although John Boulter, Dai Francis and Tony Mercer could safely walk the streets without being mobbed (unless they were in full make-up).

* * * *

During my time, there were a couple of mishaps, mainly to do with what would then have been called 'the white heat of technology', which has an ugly tendency to go stone cold when you least expect it. Because it was often hard to hear singers when they turned upstage, some sections of the show had to be pre-recorded (it would have been too costly to mike them all individually). George Mitchell (the conductor) and George Inns got together and did that so every night, there'd be 25 guys on stage, all miming. After a time, you couldn't blame them for getting complacent and just going through the motions with their minds on more important things like what they're having for tea. They didn't have to do anything arduous like sing. There were two great Western Electric generators in harness and a lowly Ferrograph on standby in case the first two went down. But that was an unlikely scenario. Even more unlikely was the prospect of all three failing at once.

One night, they did.

I was waiting to go on when it happened and the scene on stage was like a petrified forest, all silent but for a fourth tenor right at the back trying to save the show by bursting into strangulated song. He sounded about as good as Spike's prima donna with the mike on her stomach. By now, I was on the floor in convulsions and beckoning Crowther to come and have a look. Then the tape started up again in a different place and, within a few bars, they were back to the old mime routine and wondering what was for tea.

On another occasion, Leslie, Margo and I had just come off stage after lampooning a popular singing group of the time called The Kaye Sisters (I played the one with the moustache). We were still climbing out of our dresses and looking forward to a ten-minute breather when Battersea Power Station decided to take one too. In the darkness, I could hear cries of,

"George, quick! Grab your trombone and get on stage!"

So with Leslie in tow, I found my way on somehow. We couldn't see a thing and no mikes were working so I shouted to the audience,

"Join in if you know the choruses"

and began a mini-marathon of playing, bathed only in the flare of Leslie Crowther's cigarette lighter. Midway through *Alexander's Ragtime Band*, the lights came back on and the crowd went wild. I'd love to think it was in appreciation of our stalwart efforts in saving the show, but I fear it had more to do with the fact that, in the commotion, we'd rushed on stage in our underpants.

Still, it could have been worse: at least the pants were on.

Revisiting his roots in Glasgow: George on slide trombone, kids on slide.

Chapter Ten

HE NEVER WENT AWAY

...in which the gentleman returns to jazz but finds the phone has stopped ringing.

The hilarity of watching a chorus of grown Minstrels grind to a halt due to a power failure and the opportunity to become the world's first nearly nude trombonist stand out as rare moments of excitement in the otherwise brain-numbing routine of a long-running stage show. This is what I can't understand about actors: the ultimate goal for many of them is a part in a West End play with the staying power of *No Sex Please, It's Caught In The Mousetrap*. Three years of Minstrelcy at the Victoria Palace was the most I served and there were rare nights of sanity when I got time off for good behaviour. And then there was the night I took off to see Milligan.

He was appearing in a typically surreal opus called *The Bed-Sitting Room* which he'd co-written with John Antrobus. The plot was about as easy to follow as directions in Hampton Court maze but basically it dealt with a post-nuclear situation where many of the characters were mutating into inanimate objects, so it was possible for someone to play the title role. This distinction fell to an actor best known for his radio triumph as 'The Man In Black', Valentine Dyall. In the first act, he appeared as Lord Fortnum of Alamein but during the interval he metamorphosed into Lord Fortnum the room, later to become Lord Fortnum the well-known room. Graham Stark was cast as the play's equivalent of Neddy Seagoon, an heroic idiot called Captain Pontius Kak, and other comic stalwarts like Bob Todd, John Bluthal and the diminutive Johnny Vyvyan assumed a variety of roles including an underwater vicar. The music was provided by the Temperance Seven (who else?!) and Spike was in one of his favourite incarnations, the cantankerous Cockney petty official known simply as 'Mate'.

Etta and I had made the mistake of sitting quite near the front, amid the American tourists. I should have known better than to think Spike would be too engrossed in the action to notice me. That night, the only action he was engrossed in was the public humiliation of the person in charge of props who'd failed to change the Milligan drinking water from the previous performance. He was so intent on getting the audience on his side over this issue that he came to the edge of the proscenium to ask us directly if we would put up with it. It was then that he saw me. The sight of my petrified Scottish face put all thoughts of dirty drinking water from his mind and he launched into a medley of Caledonian gibberish before insisting that I come up and join him on stage. Not likely, I thought, it's my night off!

Besides, there's no greater punishment on this earth than being dragged into the spotlight when someone else is in control. If you try and top them, you're in danger of doubling the amount of egg on your face, so you just have to stand there and take the embarrassment with a smile that'll hopefully make the rest of the audience think you're not hating it. And sadly, once someone (especially someone like Mr. Milligan) decides you're going to get up and join in, there's not much you can do about it.

To be press-ganged into taking part was one thing, but to be deserted by Spike the moment I got there was quite another. I didn't know the play so I had no idea what was coming next and all I could see was the tail of Spike's threadbare Mate overcoat retreating into the wings. All the other cast members whose characters hadn't been turned into items on the props list were there with me but I drew no com-fort from this, mainly because they all seemed to be looking at me as if it were my turn to speak! I don't know if they thought Spike and I had cooked this up to confuse them but it became obvious that they were waiting for the next line before the plot could advance any further - and as Spike wasn't there and I was, they expected it to come from me. Oh Gawwwwd!!! I'm told by actors that this is the stuff recurring nightmares are made of - sod the night-mare, this was real! Well, I knew I had to do <u>something</u> so I looked round for a prop to help me out. There's never a trombone about when you need one but there was a voluptuous blonde woman in a low-cut Hungarian blouse sitting up in bed. Purely in the interests of art, I decided to join her. All eyes were still on me as I spotted a hairy false hand which I quickly seized and proceeded to muck about with. Part of the mucking about involved using the hand to grope the well-endowed blonde - well, it was a desperate situation!

Quite understandably, she began to scream and, down in the stalls, poor Etta wasn't too delighted about it either. At this point, God must have decided we'd all suffered enough because He cued the stage manager to bring the curtain down. The dismayed audience started applauding (possibly from a sense of relief) and the almost-as-dismayed cast gathered me into the line-up for the curtain call. This must have led everyone in the building apart from Etta, Spike and me to think my involvement had been deliberate. It was time for Milligan and me to have a little talk! But where was he? The moment when he was due to take his bow came and went without him. Further enquiries revealed that he was last seen on his way to his dressing-room. Right!

* * * *

"What do you mean, he's not seeing anyone tonight?", I demanded of the burly commissionaire posted outside.

"Sorry sir, Mr. Milligan has given strict instructions not to be disturbed."

A bit late for that, I thought. But short of waiting around all night for him to come out of hiding, I simply had to leave it like that. No further mention of the incident was ever made by either of us and to this day there are probably some theatre-going American ex-tourists regaling the folks back home with stories of how progressive British drama is.

* * * *

My first inkling that the three-and-a-half years I'd spent in the Victoria Palace show were probably enough came when I was walking past the theatre one Saturday night, looking forward to a day off, and a fellow came up to me and said,

"What are you doing now?"

He might as well have asked, 'Excuse me, mister, didn't you used to be George Chisholm?', particularly as we were standing beneath a 25-foot high blow-up of all the principals from the Minstrel show, self included! That's when it struck me that, although the show and my part in it had been very successful, here I was, buried alive in Victoria Street. Everyone from the jazz world seemed to think I'd deserted the business because six nights a week at the theatre and often a TV recording on Sunday left me with no time to play in clubs. It was time to get out.

So get out I did, and Max Jones (who was still writing for the *Melody Maker* at that point) did an article saying "He's back!" - I felt like saying 'He never went away! The phone didn't ring, that was all'.

In fact, when I began the Minstrels stint, I came in for copious amounts of stick from that Ku Klux Klan of the jazz world, the purists. I had to put up with cries of "Traitor!" and similar rubbish, and I was tempted to reply, 'It's okay for you. Your dad runs the local bus company, but I've got to pay the rent.'

Eventually though, the phone did start ringing again and I was being asked if I could do the So-and-so Jazz Club on the 24th and when I got there, the purists would come up and say,

"What about doing one of those wacky ratatata numbers in a striped jersey and a George Robey hat?"

Were these the same people whose previous utterance on the subject of Chisholm was 'Traitor'? Still, it goes to prove an important point about jazz: that it has to be fun. There's no need to make it serious and sepulchral; no matter how well you play, you'll drive people away if you do. The first time I saw the Modern Jazz

Quartet on stage, I thought I was in the wrong building. With their dour faces and three-quarter length frock-coats, they looked like they were at an undertakers' convention. Now there's no doubt that they play beautifully, but the feel is more like that of a chamber recital than anything to do with the spirit of New Orleans. For me, the trick is to have audiences coming away saying, 'Well if that's jazz, it's fun. I'll be back for more!'

That's very much the type of response I've tried to bring out in people throughout all these decades of freelance gigging. I've been lucky enough to combine the jazz dates with radio and TV guest spots as well as the odd film (sometimes very odd). We're not talking starring roles here, I've always been more of a cameo artiste (bit player), but the dedicated, unblinking buff might have spotted me as a wine waiter in *The Mouse on the Moon*, a sequel to *The Mouse That Roared*, in which David Kossoff and Bernard Cribbins beat America and Russia in the lunar race and proudly placed the duchy of Grand Fenwick's flag on the moon's surface. They got there by means of an unusual brand of rocket fuel discovered inside a wine bottle served by me. I remember having to react as the uncorked liquid frothed and bubbled its way out of the bottle. Reacting was my main function in films. It's a pity they don't give Oscars for it. Mind you, I have heard it said that top stars like Audrey Hepburn and Michael Caine have it written into their contracts that they get to hang on to all the fabulous designer costumes they've worn in a film. Maybe I should have insisted on keeping the wine waiter's jacket.

The Mouse On The Moon was directed by Dick Lester, a year before he made *A Hard Day's Night* and his name, in that order. One of his earliest pictures was a short called *The Running, Jumping, Standing Still Film* which achieved the near-impossible by getting the humour of the Goons to work in vision almost as well as it did in sound. Fortunately, he seemed to like casting me in small character roles, doing my reacting. In

1965, he made *The Knack* and I was called upon again, this time to don the uniform of a railway porter (I didn't keep that one either) and 'react' as Rita Tushingham made various abortive attempts to get to grips with a stubborn left luggage compartment. I was so convincing as an unhelpful attendant, I'm amazed British Rail didn't give me a job. But one Dick Lester film I didn't appear in was his version of *The Bed-Sitting Room*. I didn't go to see it either, for fear that Milligan's hand would reach out of the screen and drag me into it!

∗ ∗ ∗ ∗

TV guest spots came up pretty regularly through the 60s and 70s. On BBC1, the big Saturday night variety show was in existence for most of that time and I often cropped up on *The Billy Cotton Band Show* which took that spot in turn with the Minstrels and Val Doonican. I had a lot of time for Billy, and for Joe Loss too, because they kept as big a band as was economically possible for as long as they could. They were very loth ever to sack anyone. The oldest guy in Billy's band would just be given the cymbals to clash but it meant he was still working. One of the featured Cotton vocalists was Alan Breeze (no relation to the aforementioned Eric), the possessor of the most dreadful stammer imaginable. The only way he could get rid of it was by singing. This meant that whenever he had lines to say in the show, he'd half-sing them. Anyone who didn't know why he was doing this must have assumed he had some kind of surreal delivery. I'm surprised he didn't get an Arts Council grant.

ITV's big variety night was Sunday when Val Parnell staged his London Palladium show. I cropped up on one of these, helping the host, Bruce Forsyth, to assess a number of amateur trombonists and award them marks out of ten for spitting into the right hole. It was such a prestigious show that visiting American stars would almost always top the bill. Some even made the journey just for that one appearance. When Jack Benny came over, someone had the idea of getting the Happy Wanderers to join him. Weekend visitors to London's West End won't need reminding that these merry peak-capped troubadours could be seen (and heard!) parading through the streets like an ensemble of mobile buskers. Their fund-collecting tactics were lethal and if ever I ran into them, I knew it was going to cost me a fiver at least. It'd be,

"Hiya George, there's something wrong with me slide, look!" and the trombonist would be have the cheek to start showing me his 'faulty' slide.

"Are you aware," I used to say, "that I've only got a Boosey and Hawkes trombone, whereas you've got a Conn Conqueror?!"

This was the Rolls Royce of trombones. In fact, it was better than that. You don't get much of a tone by blowing through a Rolls Royce. Anyway, after a while I decided I'd walk on the other side of Oxford Street...which I did, only to find there's another guy there with a collecting-box. No wonder the trombonist could afford a Conn Conqueror!

When the Palladium people app-roached them about teaming up with Jack Benny, they were probably expecting a grateful 'Yes please' but instead the Wan-derers wanted to know what it would entail. When told they'd be needed for rehearsal on Saturday, they said,

"Oh, can't do Saturday. We're doing Oxford Street."

I doubt if any of the show's previous guests had turned them down with a rea-son like that; but undaunted, the Palladium folk were prepared to let them skip the rehearsal and simply turn up on the Sunday.

"Oh, can't do Sunday. We're doing Regent Street."

So that was that: the Wanderers busked in Regent Street and Jack Benny made do with the pit band!

Kids' TV has been a good source of employment for me over the last thirty-odd years, thanks early on to *Crackerjack* in which I was reunited with Leslie Crowther, and later to BBC2's *Playaway* with Brian Cant. Quite often I'd appear in sketches with Brian as well as playing a few numbers with the band led by Jonathan Cohen. The sketches were daft stuff and fun to do: the only one I can remember had a western setting in which Brian, Derek Griffiths and I were three tough gunslingers (to picture that, you'll really have to use your imagination). Brian announced that he was called Lou because he came from Louisiana, Derek told us his name was Tex because he hailed from Texas. I was highly reluctant to reveal my name, so they asked me where I came from, to which I replied,

"Maryland."

It was a short step from (hopefully) amusing the small people on the screen to (hopefully) amusing them on stage, but the main differences are to do with energy and money. On telly, you get a fair wedge for what's usually a single day's work. In panto, you get the thin end of the wedge for a schedule that would leave Seb Coe breathless. In all, I did four pantos and my memories of those tiring Christmases include throwing the villain, wrestler Jackie 'Mr. TV' Pallo to the ground (all I did was give his arm a tug, he did the rest), kissing ventriloquist Peter Brough's daughter-in-law Ayesha in an extremely desirable place (Norwich) and appearing twice as the Dame, but never shaving off the moustache. Well, for one thing, Etta wouldn't let me and anyway I couldn't go in for the full drag, I mean how do you play the trombone with a mouth full of lipstick? Well, I'm sure the Ivy Benson girls must have managed it somehow but it was beyond me. So there I was as the hirsute Dame, appealing to a new kind of public (probably the Vice Squad).

* * * *

But I wouldn't have you think the old recording career was being neglected. Far from it; I was busier in the studio than ever, mainly as a session man. It's an interesting and varied life: one day you're playing music, the next it's rock and roll. In the early 60s, I worked on an album at EMI fronted by a very popular singer of the day - I think the day was Wednesday. We arrived to find that our charts for the number *Mean To Me*, which should have been arranged in A flat, were in the key of C. Now there was a good reason for this: it was the only key the arranger could write in. So the first thing we had to do was transpose it. Still, it passed the time till the star turned up. When eventually he did arrive, he was accompanied by the impresario who treated us to a selection of expressions he'd obviously heard other people use in recording studios. They probably didn't know the meaning of them either. The first of these was,

"Let's run it down!"

As it was, there were a number of ways in which we'd happily have run it down, but we guessed he meant play the melody, so we did. Then he offered us another choice phrase,

"Can we hear the rhythm section?"

At a guess, he didn't have the remotest clue as to why he needed to hear the rhythm section; nevertheless the boys obliged. Then he decided he wanted it louder. This wasn't easy for Dave Goldberg who was playing an acoustic guitar! But Dave's an accommodating sort of bloke so he gave the strings a bit more welly. No, this still wasn't enough. So Dave, white-knuckled from applying extra plectrum pressure, gave it his all and then some. Surely the impresario would balk at the level of distortion.

"That's great," he said.

The next problem was that our singing star couldn't pitch the middle section without lapsing into a sort of Jimmy

James castrato which was hardly appropriate for this number. The impresario was highly embarrassed by this (though not as highly as the singer) and another take was called for. Unfortunately for any dogs or bats within range of Abbey Road, the same thing happened again. The singer, incensed at this rather public admission of failure, did what any star would have done in the circumstances: he threw a tantrum.

"Either we did it my way or we don't do it at all!"

These words had echoes for me (and for you if you remember Chapter 7) of Frank Sinatra, but there the similarity ended. So we had to re-arrange all the parts to fit his impression of how the piece should sound. It was a mess - and the bloody thing became a hit! That's the kind of incident that makes you wonder who should be wearing the white coats and who the straitjackets.

Tommy McQuater, my trumpeting pal (and I mean that in the nicest sense), turned out for a similar recording session one day and waited patiently for the star (whom we'll call Stella) to put in an appearance. Eventually, the producer popped into the studio to inform Tommy and the others that he'd just had a phone call to say that Stella's ill and can't sing. Quick as a flash, McQuater pipes up,

"The first of these is news."

* * * *

Sessions, though, are essential fodder if a musician has any aspirations towards eating. Sometimes they can bring you together with the great names of jazz, as happened in 1968 when I was booked to work at Philips' studio on a small group recording date with the King of Swing, Benny Goodman. Unlike some grandiose nicknames, this one was no misnomer: Benny really had been at the forefront of the swing era in the mid-1930s when the audiences went so wild that one time he and the band stopped playing, sat on the stage and watched <u>them</u>! Needless to say, the other guys and I were really looking forward to working with him. Benny arrived slightly late with a small cloth-covered hold-all containing a clarinet, an apple and a banana. I thought, 'Surely he's not going to play the banana'. I was right: he played the apple instead. Then he expressed his partiality for the work of The Beatles and how keen he was on wacky choruses. He turned to me at one point and said,

"You've got a solo there, I want you to play it funny."

I asked what he meant, fearing the worst.

"You know, ratatatata-ratata!"

I thought, 'No way am I going to do that', all too conscious of the fact that if I did and the record got issued, the dreaded puritans would come up to me and say,

"Couldn't you be serious just for once?! Mucking about on a Benny Goodman session indeed! Sacrilege!"

As it turned out, of that whole session I was only able to blow on one number, a dreadful cod Dixie version of *Octopus's Garden* which grieved me greatly. Talk about a missed opportunity! I'm told that at record fairs, copies of that disc now change hands for as much as 5p. If you paid that dearly for it, my apologies.

* * * *

Of course, I don't object to being funny when the project's a comedy album. In fact, I find it helps. That same year (1968, do pay attention), I assembled a backing group named The Inmates for an LP called *Clinton The Clown* featuring...no, not Bill Clinton but that star of the BBC Light Programme and latter-day hotelier, Clinton Ford (real name: George Harrison). It was a great opportunity to muck about with daft old numbers like *Burlington Bertie*, *When It's Night Time In Italy, It's Wednesday Over Here*, slightly newer daft numbers like *The Old Bazaar In Cairo* (one of Clinton's own, along with Ken Morris and the comedian Charlie

Chester) and more recent daft numbers like *My Baby's Wild About My Old Trombone* which Johnny Stevens cleverly managed to make sound like an old music-hall piece. I thoroughly enjoyed arranging it and had just as much fun seeing Clinton trying to sing it with a straight face. The middle section usually got him and we had to do three takes before he could get all the way through it. Basically, it's the sorry tale of a man who has been left an old trombone by his grandpapa, but alas the woman in his life seems more taken with his horn than with him. She even plays it in the ladies' powder-room! Type-casting being what it is, I played the girl playing the trombone, again without removing the 'tache. I keep thinking I must nick that one and incorporate it into the stage act.

But I guess one of the most significant developments for me on the recording scene has been the formation of the Gentlemen of Jazz (a purely snobbish title, of course). By their names shall we know them...and you won't better this line-up: Tommy Whittle on tenor saxophone, Henry MacKenzie on clarinet and alto sax. On trumpet it varies: sometimes we have Eddie Blair and sometimes Dave Hancock. Brian Lemon's the pianist, Lennie Bush is on bass, Bobby Orr's at the drums and Jack Emblow's on accordion. You might wonder what an accordionist is doing in a jazz group - at times Jack probably wonders that himself - but hearing him immediately puts all misgivings from your mind. Mind you, seeing his baby face has you wondering if he was Dorian Gray in a former life!

We didn't consciously come together as a band: at the time, we were all <u>un</u>conscious. I'd got a gig and I rang them individually, the partnership gelled and we sort of fell into the pattern of working together whenever possible. I suppose the real reason we called ourselves the Gentlemen of Jazz was to dispel the image too many people have of jazzers as a bunch of clock-watching ruffians who can't be bothered to do an extra take if something needs improvement. The truth is that jazz isn't an area of music you go into in order to make a packet - you'd soon go into liquidation if you did! Those of us who play it actually care enough to want to make it as good as possible.

So far, the Gents' recording career has included numerous sets for BBC Radio 2's *Sounds Of Jazz* (produced by Keith Stewart who never quite gets round to retiring and hosted by the late and much-missed Peter Clayton) as well as its successor, *Jazz Parade*, introduced by Britain's cheeriest trumpeter, Digby Fairweather. And there have been a couple of albums too for Bert Wilcox's Zodiac label. If you haven't heard us and you're wondering about the style, it's not dangerously progressive stuff, neither is it 'mouldy old fig' music; it's sort of somewhere in the middle. The nearest equivalent I can think of is the kind of sound John Kirby's band produced. And if you're wondering what they sounded like, well, they were rather like the Gentlemen of Jazz. I'm glad we've cleared that up.

Hopefully we strike a reasonable-ish balance between standards and new material. You can't go putting too many originals in because people complain they don't know the tune, but I try to write stuff that's as catchy as possible so that it doesn't take too much getting used to. So far, all the new numbers have come from me - I shall have to have a word with them about that! Mind you, as I'm the one getting the royalties, maybe I should keep quiet. Or perhaps I'll do what the publishers do. The publishers say,

"Yes, we'll take half the royalties for that. We'll publish it."

So they row themselves in, happily take the money, not bother to publish it, and there it stays on the shelf dying of old age. My standard response to publishers now is,

"No thanks very much, I'd rather have twelve twelfths of the money, rather than the six twelfths you're offering me."

Sentimental old fool that I am.

We were able to combine the elements of live and recorded performance in 1980 when Bryan Izzard at Scottish Television produced a series of six shows, simply entitled *The Jazz Series* (I believe it took a team of 20 creative consultants to think that one up). The idea was to have the Gentlemen of Jazz as a regular fixture, playing a total of about half a dozen numbers each week (usually standards) and for me to introduce a whole range of guests who would reflect the various aspects of music all of which come under the 'jazz' umbrella. So it was that we could feature artists as diverse as saxophonist Kathy Stobart, singer Carol Kidd, acoustic guitarist John Williams, those jazz-funksters Morrisey Mullen and the modern Scots band Head, all in the same series. Sadly, the show was only seen in Scotland and we never got a second run but it's good to have been involved in one of TV's all-too-rare forays into jazz.

Casting an eye over these last few pages tires me out when I realise how busy I'd been up to and including the early 1980s. In the light of that, I suppose I was lucky it didn't happen on stage. Instead, it happened at home.

Etta and I had moved to a part of Bedfordshire called Silsoe and over the Christmas of 1982, I began doing the decorating. The action of stretching to put up one of those long strips of wallpaper was suddenly accompanied by a feeling of indescribable fatigue and a furious heartbeat thumping away in a time signature even Buddy Rich would have found hard to keep up with. That was what was happening as far as I was concerned. The medical definition was that I was having a coronary.

The Chisholms pop in at the Palace.

L to R: Garry, Etta, George and Carole.

Chapter Eleven

A HEART IN THE RIGHT PLACE

…in which George conquers his ailments, is honoured for services to jazz and reaches his biggest audience yet.

"What do you do for a living?" asked the doctor.

It was almost as flattering an enquiry as the one made by that passer-by outside the Victoria Palace in the 60s ("What are you doing now?"). I had hoped that, by the beginning of 1983, the face and the name might have meant something, even to a heart specialist. Maybe his set was permanently tuned to *Casualty*.

Still, this was no time to be vain - though that didn't stop me. The good quack was merely trying to gauge whether I'd be able to work again and, if so, how soon and to what extent. He needed to know which line of employment I was in before he could calculate how much heart-stress might be involved. So, helpful as ever, I told him I blew down a brass pipe. I couldn't have met with a more mirthless reaction if I'd been playing the first house on a Monday night at the Glasgow Empire. When we'd established the nature of the brass pipe in question, he dived head-first into his library of medical thomes only to discover that - surprise surprise - there was nothing in any of them which covered trombone players. Hod carriers, yes - but trombonists, no. It struck me as a little late in the day to make the switch to hod-carrying (though some may have seen it as a good career move) so we just had to resort to a common-sense prescription: if it hurts, stop. I suppose that applies as a good rule-of-thumb to just about anything in life. With that in mind, I started practising again (not in his surgery, I waited till I got home) and although my health gradually improved, I began getting angina pains in the arm, across the chest and down the other arm.

The funny part was that whenever I blew the trombone, the pain went away! That piece of information came as quite a shock to my chum, the mirthless medic. When I told him, he looked utterly startled, called all the other specialists in and said,

"Pain goes away when he's playing

trombone!"

I'm not sure how pleased he was about this: I think he may have had a nightmare vision of a hospital with cubicles full of patients all playing trombones. Not a bad idea in my view: they could have made it an extension to the hod-carriers' ward.

But think how lucky I'd been. At the time when I was having the attack, I didn't have a clue how serious it was. I just knew something was going on and I didn't like it. And the actual surgery happened without my really knowing what was involved. Just as well, if you ask me, because having experienced it I then had people coming up to me and saying,

"You've done terribly well!"

"Why?" I innocently enquired, then wished I hadn't because this would lead to a graphic description of a major heart by-pass operation. And in my case, it was a triple by-pass (can't think why, I'm not a civil servant). When it hit me as to just what that meant, I went,

"Chrrr-ist!"…as one does in such situations.

Unbeknown to me at the time, a good pal of mine, Len Skeat the bass player, had the kind thought of going up to see poor old George in hospital. But really it was too soon after the surgery: I was still in the intensive care ward, hooked up to a machine with tubes coming out of practically every orifice - and there are several, folks: two down the throat, up your nostrils, in your ears, everywhere. So poor Len troops up, innocently asks if he can see George Chisholm and of course the nurse shouldn't have let him in, but instead she said,

"Yes, he's in there."

She directed him into intensive care where I lay, oblivious of the whole scene (thank God) amid a gruesome network of tubes, looking for all the world like a 3D map of the London Underground. Len took one look and felt so ill, he nearly needed to join me! But thanks anyway, Len.

Recuperation's a slow and patience-testing business and I still get angina pains today, so I've had to learn to live with it. But then, that's better than learning to die with it, so I'm not complaining. The only thing I will say is that after the day I got by-passed more times than Croydon, the good Doctor Mirthless assured me that was me fixed up for life, no five thousand mile service (and hopefully for a long time, no memorial service) but then along came the angina. I rest my case - I have to, it's exhausted.

* * * *

Through a happy accident of timing, though, while I was clawing my way back to some semblance of health, I was probably reaching a wider public than ever before.

Prior to falling ill, I'd been hired by Dick Lester to display another bout of cinematic reacting in one of his epics. This time it was *Superman 3*, the one in which the baddies got to him and made him do all sorts of evil deeds, one of them being to straighten the Tower of Pisa. Not exactly on a par with the bombing of Hiroshima, I grant you, but it didn't half cramp John Bluthal's style. John was playing a street vendor whose stock-in-trade was plastic models of the leaning tower and he wasn't at all amused to see the course of geography change in an instant. My role was that of a Pisan road-sweeper and I was required to stand with John and, yes, 'react' as Christopher Reeve supposedly put the tower at right angles to the ground. Glamorous stuff, until you realise that John and I were being filmed alone in Elstree with just an eye-line to follow.

All the same, I was pretty chuffed to know that John and I would be virtually the last faces on the screen because at the end of the picture, after Superman's recovered from his bout of baddiness, he rushes round the world like a last-minute Christmas shopper, desperately righting all his earlier wrongs. At the eleventh hour, he remembers Pisa and again I stood there 'reacting' as Bluthal got even more furious: he'd just started flogging straight tower models!

So while I was preparing to rejoin the living after my little sojourn in intensive care, my mug was on show all over the country, and mainly to an audience of kids. Obviously that was good in some ways, but it had its drawbacks.

"Wow! You were in *Superman*?", marvelled the kids.

"Yea, but I'm really a jazz musician."

"What's he like?"

"Who?"

"Superman, of course!"

"Oh, well I never actually met him. We were just given this eye-line to follow. Anyway, let me tell you about when I played the middle eight of *Laura*..."

"Never mind Laura, what about Lois Lane?"

And I don't think they meant the singer.

* * * *

After what had happened last time, I never went near decorating again. Perhaps it was God's way of telling me I simply wasn't house-trained. But it had never occurred to me that someone else might have had the idea of decorating me. Granted, a spot of artex on the eyebrows and a strip of wall-paper over the moustache may have been an improvement, but the decoration turned out to be an OBE.

When they notified me about this, I was delighted to be told it was being award-ed for services to jazz, not for services to wearing a George Robey hat and a stripey jumper. As far as I'm aware, getting the gong for services to jazz is a bit of a rarity. The only other person I know who's got one is Ronnie Scott. Well, they were hardly going to give him one for services to jokes!

Perhaps it's kept as a marginal category for fear that if all the retired colonels heard about it - and someone explained to them what jazz is - there might be a repeat of the mid-60s occasion when a whole battalion of them returned their decorations in protest at the ennoblement of The Beatles. Still, I suppose the palace would just melt them down and make new ones.

For anything that involves meeting royalty, it's essential to know 'the form'. Never having received an OBE before, I wasn't sure if there was any kneeling to be done, but luckily the Queen and I were both spared the sight of an arthritic Chis desperately trying to unlock his joints and get perpendicular again. If the worst had come to the worst, I suppose one of the footmen could have provided a little trolley, slid it under me and wheeled me away with a cry of 'Next please!' - but no, kneeling was not necessary. However, I was given strict instructions only to speak if Her Majesty spoke to me.

I think I could have worked that one out for myself. Honestly, what did they think I was going to do, ask her for a date?

"Er, pardon me, Your Queenship, but if you're not doing anything later, d'you fancy a couple of jars down the British Legion?"

Can't really see it, can you? Anyway, I prefer older women and her mother was washing her crown that night.

As it turned out, she did speak to me. I was terrified it was going to be another variation of that all-too-regular question,

"And what do you do?"

but she seemed to know what I did because she asked how long I' d been playing the trombone. Coincidentally, the ceremony was taking place in the very same ballroom at Buckingham Palace where I'd performed in the late 30s so I was able to say to her,

"Well you see that little balcony up

there? I used to play there with Ambrose's band, many years ago, when you were only that high and you and your sister were allowed to pop in and see all the bright lights and people dancing."

"Oh you must have been playing a long time," she observed.

I resisted the temptation to riposte that I did get a tea-break in about 1942. Instead we just shook hands, she gave me the gong and that was it. Exciting stuff for me (and gratifying too) but the people who really went wild over it were the Americans.

The jazz impresario Dick Gibson invited me over to Colorado to take part in one of his conventions and when news of this OBE thing leaked out, it caused a certain amount of confusion over points of etiquette. Ludicrously, a lot of the men had taken to calling me 'Sir George'. I'm surprised they didn't ask where my suit of armour had gone. And the women got themselves in a twist over whether or not they should curtsey to me! Looking back, I should have milked the situation for all it was worth, insisted on red carpets, stretch limos and a private plane to take me from the dressing-room to the stage. But I suppose the misplaced title was thrill enough. It made me feel like a jazz knight, entering the realm of musical aristocracy that already contained Count Basie, Duke Ellington and someone with whom I was due to be reunited, Benny 'King' Carter.

Benny was another of Dick Gibson's guests, well into his 70s by then and blowing better than ever. It was exhilarating playing with him again after nearly half a century and I was equally thrilled to be blowing alongside other American greats such as trumpeter Billy Butterfield, Satchmo's old trombonist Trummy Young (who died soon after) and the tenor saxophonist Scott Hamilton who was only in his 30s but had the maturity of style of a much older musician.

Dick's jazz parties were an annual event and I was invited back to do, amongst other things, an anecdotal spot. It was nice to be thought of as amusing and witty <u>within</u> a jazz context, rather than having to convince people that my main role in life is to play jazz, not just do gags.

* * * *

Alas, not all Americans appreciate my humour. If they did, I'd still be there, but I can think of at least one major US jazzer who could rival my old heart specialist for mirthlessness: Ruby Braff.

Ruby had buttonholed me at one of the Gibson parties in Denver, said he was visiting England soon to play at the Pizza Express in Dean Street and that he wanted me to come down and blow with him. It isn't something I would normally do because generally there's nothing worse than turning up at a venue like that with the trombone and asking 'Mind if I sit in?', but as I'd been specifically invited and as Ruby's such a good player, I went against my better judgement just the once. Besides, I was honour-bound: Jim Douglas had also been asked to go and his car had broken down so he needed a lift. So that was settled.

When we turned up, Ruby failed to acknowledge us as he was a little too busy effing and blinding over the state of the air-conditioning. He went the whole of the first set without inviting us on at any time so, giving him the benefit of the doubt, I reasoned that he must have been saving us up for later. A mixed blessing, it seemed, from the curtness with which he treated his rhythm section (a good one including Kenny Baldock and Brian Lemon). Well, the evening progressed…which is more than I did. This unplayed trombone at my feet seemed to be getting bigger and bigger - maybe I was just getting smaller and smaller. If it had been Jack Teagarden up there, I would probably have wept but as it was, I was all for saying 'Stuff it'. I put this viewpoint to Jim, suggesting that we leave immediately. That turned out to be impossible as Ruby had just asked Jim to get up and play! I was beginning to wonder whether, along with angina, I'd also contracted invisibility when Braff extended a polite invitation to me along the lines of,

"What are you f***ing sitting there for? Get on the f***ing stage!"

For this, he nearly got a Boosey and Hawkes trombone wrapped round his bonce (a goodly footage of metal, I might add) but I forbore and joined him.

Not surprisingly, he proved to be an extremely competitive customer and he didn't like it when I responded to the little musical quotes he threw at me and got a good reaction from the audience. At one point, he let me loose on one of those 95 chorus jobs, no doubt looking forward to the collapse of Chis in mid-solo. But I got through it by using the old trick of pointing the trombone slide towards the floor for the low notes, straight ahead for the mid-range and high in the air for the top ones. Again, he wasn't very pleased but on those rare occasions when he did smile, I realised he reminded me of someone, though I couldn't think who. A little man, his square face, fringe of hair and clown-like grin were definitely familiar. I told him so and I think he expected me to exclaim, 'I've got it: Jesus Christ!' instead of which I suddenly realised and said,

"I've got it: Alfie Bass!"

"Alfie Bass?" he pondered, never having heard of him. "Is he good?"

"Oh Ruby, he's the best at what he does."

This seemed to please him more than most of what I'd done that night, but God help me if he ever finds out that what Alfie Bass did do was specialise in playing hapless army privates in low-budget war films and TV sitcoms!

* * * *

With all the anxieties over the state of my own health, I find it cruelly ironic that it was Etta who went first. In the summer of 1990, she died suddenly of cancer and it has been very difficult for me to adjust because we were so close. I sometimes wish I had cried properly at the time. I didn't because there were people there and I didn't want them to see me break down. It might have been better if I had because it was a delayed reaction thing; I just couldn't believe it. I still don't really believe it and I haven't any convictions one way or the other about life after death or reincarnation or whatever. I don't really know and I wish someone would tell me the answer. I've spoken to the religious folk and they've said,

"These people who say there is no life after death are merely making a statement. There's no proof."

But surely, equally, the people who say there IS life after death are merely expressing an opinion and there's no proof - so I don't know what to believe. I certainly wish there was. I'd love to think that when the time comes, I can see her and we can live happily ever after.

In the meantime, I console myself

with the cliché that life goes on. My daughter Carole and her husband Don and their two sons now live with me, and I live with my ailments. I have tablets to control the angina so at least there's no pain any more but, heigh ho, I've now gone and got diabetes. I began to realise something was wrong when my trombone-playing started to go slightly awry. I'm very critical of my own work and although other people said it sounded fine to them, I wasn't convinced. I didn't have enough puff in me, I had a very dry mouth and I was visiting the bathroom far too often (we're talking number ones here, folks, for those of you that take an interest in such things). So I went to the specialist who did all the tests - blood and urine samples - and came back and said,

"I'll kill that cat!"

but the basic upshot was that I'd got sugar in my blood, so I asked,

"Is there any blood in my blood?"

He went on to explain that this

meant I was diabetic. Immediately, I entertained horrific visions of being arrested as a suspected junkie, having to ape Billie Holiday and wear long evening gloves to hide the needle marks or worst of all walking about with this needle saying, 'I haven't got another hole in my body to put this needle in. What do I do now?' Luckily though, pills keep it under control so I'm not in danger of being punctured. I have to keep to a strictly disciplined diet, of course, and sweet things are out. I don't know if this applies to playing sentimental ballads but I'd better keep off them just in case.

* * * *

Thank God I am well enough to work because the BBC appear to have reminded themselves of me and lately I've been on the radio almost as often as the pips.

I was invited to show off my lack of knowledge as a panellist on Benny Green's *Jazz Score* as well as guesting on *Bob Holness Requests The Pleasure*, performing a jokey routine with Bob which involved getting steadily legless…though perhaps 'steadily' is not the word. I had thought of doing a programme called 'George Chisholm Requests The Pleasure' but I was afraid it might be greeted with a cry of 'He'll be lucky at his age!' Mind you, I have been hosting a number of shows too. Roy Oakshott produced a record programme called *Hogmania* in which I 'saw in' 1991 and this led to six more outings of DJ Chis when Alan Dell was on holiday. Prior to that, Graham Pass had had the idea of reviving the old-style big band broadcasts in a series called *Things Are Swinging* where I introduced and played with the Radio Big Band, almost bringing me full circle in terms of my wireless career.

If I carry on at this rate, I wander how long it'll be before I'm playing the piano back in the Tower ballroom, Glasgow, and diving beneath it when the punch-ups start. You never know: perhaps Wingy will still be around to protect me!

GC with fellow musician and entertainer Roy Castle (who succeeded him as the host of Radio 2's *Things are Swinging*).

OUTRO

George died on 6th December, 1997 after a long spell at the BUPA nursing home in Milton Keynes. At the funeral one week later, John Dankworth praised the man's musicianship which he said was often overlooked in favour of the Chisholm gift for comedy; a sentiment the deceased would have agreed with.

A recording was played of George's hero, Jack Teagarden performing *One Hundred Years From Today*, its lyric urging the listener to go out and live for the present as none of what we do will matter one century on; a philosophy the deceased had practised for most of his 82 years.

Appendix 1
DESERT ISLAND DISCS

George was cast away twice on Roy Plomley's mythical island, once in 1963 and again nearly twenty years later. The second programme can be heard in full on the *DID* website and touches on his pre-trombone flirtation with the trumpet, how he interrupted his honeymoon to work with Fats Waller and the drunk act he put on in front of bandleader Lew Stone, who believed it and never hired him again.

He seemed confident that he'd be able to look after himself on a desert island and when asked if he could fish, joshed that he might just land the odd boot. Mr Plomley, it seemed, struggled to get the joke.

There were Chisholm connections elsewhere in the series' history: Leslie Crowther, George's sometime colleague, chose *My Mother's Eyes* by GC & The Tradsters when he was similarly marooned in 1962 and the great Jack Teagarden himself had been a castaway in 1957.

Desert Island Discs:

GEORGE CHISHOLM

BBC Home Service

Presented by **ROY PLOMLEY**

Producer: **MONICA CLIFFORD**

Transmission: **29.04.63**

1. BOBBY HACKETT – The Boy Next Door

2. LEONARD PENNARIO - Debussy: Arabesque No. 1

3. LOUIS ARMSTRONG – Thanks A Million

4. DENNIS BRAIN & THE PHILHARMONIA ORCHESTRA/HERBERT VON KARAJAN – Mozart: Horn Concerto No. 4 in E flat major

5. SPIKE MILLIGAN – The Sewers Of The Strand

6. ELLA FITZGERALD – I Got Rhythm

7. JACK TEAGARDEN – Don't Tell A Man About His Woman (castaway's favourite)

8. ART TATUM – Dvorak: Humoresque in G flat major, Op. 101/7

Book: An Anthology of Humour

Luxury: Trombone and hair restorer (how did he get away with having two?).

Desert Island Discs:

GEORGE CHISHOLM

BBC Radio 4

Presented by ROY PLOMLEY

Producer: DEREK DRESCHER

Transmission: 13.03.82

---

1. NAT KING COLE – Autumn Leaves

2. JAMES GALWAY & THE NATIONAL PHILHARMONIC ORCHESTRA/CHARLES GERHARDT – Bach: Flute Sonata No. 4: Allegro

3. LOUIS ARMSTRONG – Thanks A Million

4. ART TATUM – Massenet: Elegie

5. GEORGE CHISHOLM QUARTET - Blue Turning Grey Over You

6. BOBBY HACKETT – I Guess I'll Have To Change My Plan (castaway's favourite)

7. DENNIS BRAIN & THE PHILHARMONIA ORCHESTRA/WALTER SUSSKIND – Mozart: Horn Concerto No. 4 in E flat major

8. URBIE GREEN – The Look Of Love

Book: Either P.G. Wodehouse "…or some Spike Milligan ravings."

Luxury: An engraved glass and a supply of bitter lemon.

Appendix 2
JAZZ LEGENDS

Around what would have been George's 90th birthday, I was invited onto this long-running Radio 3 series for an hour celebrating the Chisholm effect. The programme's regular host, the pianist and composer Julian Joseph, proved to be a great enthusiast for George's style of playing and was able to identify with many of his experiences as a working British jazz musician.

GC with US trumpet star Billy Butterfield

Jazz Legends: GEORGE CHISHOLM

BBC Radio 3

Presented by JULIAN JOSEPH & BOB SINFIELD

Producer: KEITH LOXAM

Transmission: 08.07.05

1.
Title: PENALTY £5
Artist: GEORGE CHISHOLM
Composer: Chisholm
Publisher: MCPS
Album: British Jazz Vol.1
Label: BBC
Number: REC 143M

2.
George Chisholm interview clip from the
Omnibus television programme (VC 148084)
Original transmission 03/06/73

(GC tells of his appearance at a 'modern' jazz club where, by his own admission, he was 'playing rubbish!' yet the crowd burst into rapturous applause and yelled for more. Julian Joseph says the same thing has happened to him.)

3.
Title: HUMMIN' TO MYSELF
Artist: DUNCAN WHYTE
Composer: Magidson/Fain/Siegel
Publisher: Victoria
Album: Stars of Swing
Label: Harlequin
Number: HQ 3015 (GC on celeste)

4.
Title: TIN ROOF BLUES
Artists: THE MARK WHITE DIXIELANDERS
Composer: New Orleans Rhythm Kings
Publisher: Darewski Music
Single/EP: A Night at the Nest
Label: Decca
Number: DFE 6553

5.
Title: HOLIDAY EXPRESS
Artists: TEDDY JOYCE BAND
Composer: Macaffer
Publisher: M.C.P.S
Album: The Golden Age of British Jazz
Label: World Records
Number: SH 364

6.

Title: PARDON ME PRETTY BABY
Artist: BENNY CARTER
Composers: Klages/Maskill/Rose
Publishers: Lawrence Wright/Redwood
Album: Symphony in Riffs
Label: Academy, Sound and Vision Ltd.
Number: CD AJA 5075

7.

George Chisholm interview clip from the
Omnibus television programme (VC 148084)
Original transmission 03/06/73

(GC recalls working with Fats Waller and remarks on
the size of the man and how he used it as a joke.)

8.

Title: THE FLAT FOOT FLOOGIE
Artists: FATS WALLER AND HIS CONTINENTAL
RHYTHM
Composers: Slim Gaillard/Slam Stewart
Publisher: Worldwide
Album: The One and Only Thomas "Fats" Waller.
Label: Memoir Records
Number: CD MOIR306

9.

George Chisholm interview clip from the
Omnibus television programme (VC 148084)
Original transmission 03/06/73

(GC tells of when Ambrose was asked to play 'You Are
The One'…which turned out to be *Night And Day*.)

10.
Title: ANCHOR'S AWEIGH
Artists: THE SQUADRONAIRES
Composers: Zimmerman/Miles/Lovell
Album: There's Something in the Air
Label: Decca
Number: F8262

11.
George Chisholm interview clip from the
Jazz Score radio programme (PLN613/86LC0079)
Original transmission 13/04/86

(GC remembers Sinatra recording with the BBC Show
Band, insisting on singing in the middle of the brass
section.)

12.
Title: POLL WINNERS
Artists: KENNY BAKER'S ALL STARS
Composer: Dankworth
Publisher: Mecolico
Album: All The Winners-Melody Maker Jazz Poll 1958-
9
Label: Pye Records
Number: NJT 518

13.
George Chisholm interview clip from the *Omnibus*
television programme (VC 148084)
Original transmission 03/06/73

(GC says he hates labels: you blow into the hole and
what comes out is either good or bad.)

193

14.
George Chisholm interview clip from the Goons documentary programme,
At Last the Go On Show (VC 41SX4553)
Original transmission TX 27.5.91

(GC remembers Angela Morley's scoring which gave everyone something interesting to do. Angela then introduces a *Goon Show* clip of GC in a speaking part.)

15.
Title: ONE FOR MONK
Artists: THE GENTLEMEN OF JAZZ
Composer: George Chisholm
Album: The Swinging Mr C
Label: Zodiac
Number: ZR1026

16.
George Chisholm clip from the BBC television programme, *NYJO's World of Music* (VC194419)
Original transmission TX 03/04/78

(GC praises the National Youth Jazz Orchestra, saying the future of British jazz is in safe hands.)

17.
Title: MY MOTHER'S EYES
Artists: GEORGE CHISHOLM TRADSTERS
Composers: Gilbert/Baer
Publisher: Day
Album: Trad Treat!
Label: Wing/Polydor
Number: WL1043